Begin Hairdressing

Hairdressing And Beauty Industry Authority Series

Begin Hairdressing – The Official Guide to Level 1
Martin Green

Hairdressing: The Foundations – The Official Guide to Level 2
Leo Palladino

Professional Hairdressing – The Official Guide to Level 3
Martin Green, Lesley Kimber and Leo Palladino

Beauty Therapy: The Foundations – The Official Guide to Level 2
Lorraine Nordmann

Professional Beauty Therapy – The Official Guide to Level 3
Lorraine Nordmann, Lorraine Appleyard and Pamela Linforth

Safety in the Salon — Elaine Almond

Patrick Cameron: Dressing Long Hair — Patrick Cameron and Jackie Wadeson

Patrick Cameron: Dressing Long Hair Book 2 — Patrick Cameron

Trevor Sorbie: Visions in Hair — Trevor Sorbie, Kris Sorbie and Jacki Wadeson

Mahogany: Steps to Cutting, Colouring and Finishing Hair
Martin Gannon and Richard Thompson

The Art of Hair Colouring — David Adams and Jacki Wadeson

Bridal Hair — Pat Dixon and Jacki Wadeson

The Total Look — Ian Mistlin

Men's Hairdressing: Traditional and Modern Barbering — Maurice Lister

African-Caribbean Hairdressing — Sandra Gittens

The World of Hair and **The World of Skin Care** — Dr John Gray

Aromatherapy for the Beauty Therapist — Valerie Worwood

Indian Head Massage — Muriel Burnham-Airey and Adele O'Keefe

Manicure, Pedicure and Advanced Nail Techniques — Elaine Almond

The Complete Make-Up Artist: Working in Film, Television and Theatre
Penny Delamar

The Science of Cosmetics and **The Beauty Salon and Its Equipment**
John V Simmons

Begin Hairdressing

The Official Guide to Level 1

Martin Green

Australia • Canada • Mexico • Singapore • Spain • United Kingdom • United States

THOMSON

Begin Hairdressing: The Official Guide to Level 1 – first edition

Copyright © 2005 Thomson Learning

The Thomson logo is a registered trademark used herein under licence.

For more information contact Thomson Learning, High Holborn House, 50–51 Bedford Row, London WC1R 4LR or visit us on the World Wide Web at: http://www.thomsonlearning.co.uk

All rights reserved by Thomson Learning 2005. The text of this publication, or any part thereof, may not be reproduced or transmitted in any form or by any means, electronic or mechanical, including photocopying, recording, storage in an information retrieval system, or otherwise, without prior permission of the publisher.

While the publisher has taken all reasonable care in the preparation of this book the publisher makes no representation, express or implied, with regard to the accuracy of the information contained in this book and cannot accept any legal responsibility or liability for any errors or omissions from the book or the consequences thereof.

Products and services that are referred to in this book may be either trademarks and/or registered trademarks of their respective owners. The publishers and author make no claim to these trademarks.

British Library Cataloguing-in-Publication Data
A catalogue record for this book is available from the British Library.

ISBN 1-84480-174-8

This edition published 2005 by Thomson Learning

Design and project management by The Partnership Publishing Solutions Ltd, www.the-pps.co.uk

Printed in Great Britain by The Bath Press Ltd

Contents

Foreword viii
Preface ix
Acknowledgements x

1 Introduction 1
About this book 1
About Hairdressing NVQ Level 1 2
National Vocational Qualifications (NVQs) 4
Completing the activities 5
Under assessment 6

2 Health and safety 7
Introduction 7
    The Health and Safety at Work Act (1974) 8
    What do you need to know? 8
    Now try these out! 9
Hazard and risk 12
    Hazards of the environment 12
    Hazards to do with equipment and materials 12
    Hazards to do with people 12
    Risk assessment 13
    Now try these out! 15
A safe working environment 17
    Obstructions 17
    Spillage and breakages 17
    Now try these out! 18
    Preventing infection 19
Personal health, hygiene and appearance 21
    Hands and nails 21
    Now try these out! 22
    Your body 24
    Your mouth 24
    Personal appearance 24
    Clothes 24
    Shoes 25
    Hair 25
    Jewellery 25
    Posture 25
    Now try these out! 26
Emergencies 28
    Fire 28
    Accidents (first aid) 29
    Now try these out! 30

3 Receiving clients and making appointments 33

Introduction 33
   What do you need to know? 34
   Now try these out! 35

Maintaining reception and retail areas 36
   Now try these out! 36

Checking products and stationery 39
   Now try these out! 41

Greeting people and dealing with their enquiries 43
Taking messages 47
   Confidentiality 47
   Now try these out! 48

Making appointments 49
   If in doubt 51
   Now try these out! 51

4 Working together 55

Introduction 55
   What do you need to know? 56
   Now try these out! 57

Creating a good impression with clients 58
   Client records 59
   Late arrivals and 'on-spec' appointments 60
   Now try these out! 60

Create good working relationships with colleagues 63
   Now try these out! 65

Building on your own abilities at work 66
   Strengths and weaknesses 67
   Staff appraisal and reviews 68
   Self-appraisal 68
   Personal action (or training) plans 69
   Self-development 69
   Now try these out! 70

5 Salon duties and routines 73

Introduction 73
   What do you need to know? 74
   Now try these out! 75

Preventing infection 76
   Sterilisation 77
   Now try these out! 77

General salon hygiene and routine maintenance 79
   Trolleys and trays 79

Floors and seating   80
Work surfaces   81
Now try these out!   81
Styling mirrors   83
Salon equipment   83
Disposing of waste   85
Now try these out!   85
Finding treatment records   87

6 Shampooing and conditioning hair   89

Introduction   89
What do you need to know?   90
Now try these out!   90
Preparations   92
Now try these out!   93
Choosing a shampoo and conditioner   95
1 Hair type/texture   95
2 Conditioning benefits to the hair   95
3 The service or treatment to follow   95
Shampooing the client   96
Conditioning the client   99
Now try these out!   100

7 Helping with perms, relaxing and colour processes   103

Introduction   103
What do you need to know?   105
Now try these out!   107
Process overviews   109
Perming/neutralising   109
Relaxing hair   110
Removing colours and lighteners   110
Now try these out!   111
Working with different products   114
Neutralising   115
After a perm   115
After a relaxer   116
Colour removal   117
Removing (a single) colour from hair   117
Removing (multiple) colours from hair   119
Now try these out!   120

Appendix   125
Glossary   127
Index   132

Foreword

What do you want to do when you leave school? You probably want a role that is exciting, vibrant and varied which will lead to an interesting future.

Let Martin Green's *Begin Hairdressing* inspire you to start your qualification in hairdressing, which will bring you a rewarding and fruitful career with endless prospects for future development. With over 30 years of practical experience, Martin is an accomplished professional who's wealth of experience, knowledge and understanding of the industry shine through in this informative and comprehensive book that will become an invaluable source of guidance as you start work.

The British hairdressing industry is renowned for having the highest standards in the world and with high standards comes hard work and a determination to meet the standards of the industry and of your clients. The reward is real satisfaction when you see the results of your work in your client's hair and the real motivator and testimony to your success is when your client's look and persona is transformed by your work.

Alan Goldsbro
Chief Executive Officer
HABIA

Preface

Our life is a journey down a path with lots of possible and different destinations. Where we end up depends on the route we take. Each time we arrive at a crossroads we are confronted with choices; do we go left, do we go right or do we head straight on? In making a choice we force change to occur.

It is only natural to avoid or resist change, we often prefer relative comfort and the routines we know to making tough decisions. But, inevitably, it is indecision – the lack of ability to choose a direction or a course of action – that hampers our progress. So we have to accept the fact that, to have choice, we must accept change.

Not all choices are hard though, some are fun and some are exciting: What shall I buy today? What can I wear? Where shall we eat tonight? Where shall we go on holiday? Where can we live? Then we ask; what job can I do and will I enjoy it? The only way to find the answer to the last question is to try it out first.

The introductory level 1 NVQ in hairdressing is a great way to experience what the craft has in store for you: What does it involve? Will I like it? Where could it take me? It provides an opportunity to answer so many questions, gain valuable experience and meet lots of people while gaining a nationally recognised qualification too.

Good luck for the future.

Martin Green

Acknowledgements

The author and publishers would like to thank the following for providing images:

Wella, Lawrain Aumonier, L'Oréal Professionel, HSE, Simon Shaw at WAHL, Java for Hair, Toni & Guy, S. Lewis, BLM Health, Beiersdorf UK, Marianne Marjerus, Mahogany, Sean Hanna, Neville Daniel, Anthony Mascolo and Pat Mascolo for TiGi, Chris Moody, MICOL Direct Ltd, Peter Hickman, Ellisons, Saks, Alex Springer, Camera Press Ltd, George Paterson SA Hairdressing, Desmond Murray, Anthony Holland at Zullo & Pack, Adrian Alan and Charles Worthington.

Special thanks to HABIA for permission to use some of their copyright materials from the National Occupational Standards for hairdressing NVQ level 1 and the Official Health and Safety Implementation Pack for Hairdressers.

Other materials referenced in this book are available from the Health and Safety Executive (HSE) and HMSO.

Many thanks to Sandra Gittens, author of *African-Caribbean Hairdressing* published by Thomson Learning 2002.

Every effort has been made to trace all copyright holders, but if any have been inadvertently overlooked the publishers will be pleased to make the necessary arrangements at the first opportunity.

Introduction

About this book

This book is an all-in-one companion to help you through your Hairdressing Level 1 programme. The contents are set out in a uniform way and each topic breaks down the information you need to know into small, 'digestible' chunks. You can choose to work through these topics in any order because each one contains:

- clearly explained information that is relevant to the task
- linked activities that you can complete
- key words and phrases
- example questions and model answers
- things to remember.

About Hairdressing NVQ Level 1

The Hairdressing Level 1 NVQ (National Vocational Qualification) is made up of six units. Five of these are mandatory and one is optional:

NVQ units

Mandatory units (all units must be completed)

- **G1** Ensure your own actions reduce risks to health and safety
- **G2** Assist with salon reception duties
- **G3** Contribute to the development of effective working relationships
- **H1** Shampoo and condition hair
- **H5** Prepare for hairdressing services and maintain work areas

Plus one of the following:

Optional units (one must be completed)

- **H2** Assist with perming and colouring services
- **H3** Assist with perming, relaxing and colouring services
- **H4** Assist with perming, relaxing and colouring services for African–Caribbean hair

The illustration below shows the main objectives for each of the mandatory units, all of which must be completed. Each NVQ unit is broken down into two or more smaller parts (elements). This illustration shows the five mandatory units, their reference number, unit title and associated main outcomes or elements:

The mandatory NVQ units and elements

Unit	Title	Element	Description
G1	Ensure your own actions reduce risks to health and safety	G1.1	Identify the hazards and evaluate the risks in your workplace
		G1.2	Reduce the risks to health and safety in your workplace
G2	Assist with salon reception duties	G2.1	Maintain the reception area
		G2.2	Attend to clients and enquiries
		G2.3	Help to make appointments for salon services
G3	Contribute to the development of effective working relationships	G3.1	Develop effective working relationships with clients
		G3.2	Develop effective working relationships with colleagues
		G3.3	Develop yourself within the job role
H1	Shampoo and condition hair	H1.1	Maintain effective and safe methods of working when shampooing and conditioning hair
		H1.2	Shampoo and condition hair
H5	Prepare for hairdressing services and maintain work areas	H5.1	Prepare for salon services
		H5.2	Maintain the work area for hairdressing services

Introduction

And this illustration shows the optional units (only one of which needs to be undertaken). Again, the reference number, unit title and elements are shown:

The optional NVQ units and elements

H2	Assist with perming and colouring services	H2.1	Maintain effective and safe methods of working when assisting with perming and colouring services
		H2.2	Neutralise hair as part of the perming process
		H2.3	Remove colouring and lightening products
H3	Assist with perming, relaxing and colouring services	H3.1	Maintain effective and safe methods of working when assisting with perming relaxing and colouring services
		H3.2	Neutralise hair as part of the perming and relaxing process
		H3.3	Remove colouring and lightening products
H4	Assist with perming, relaxing and colouring services for African–Caribbean hair	H4.1	Maintain effective and safe methods of working when assisting with perming relaxing and colouring services for African–Caribbean hair
		H4.2	Neutralise hair as part of the perming and relaxing process
		H4.3	Remove colouring and lightening products

National Vocational Qualifications (NVQs)

You might have noticed from the previous illustrations that National Vocational Qualifications (NVQs) have a set format made up of:

- a unit reference number
- a unit title
- different elements, i.e. the main outcomes.

This provides a simple, at-a-glance way of identifying the related tasks. However, it does not explain what you need to understand or what is required under an assessment situation. To find this out, you need to know that each of the elements, or tasks, is broken down into the following components:

1. Performance criteria – a number of statements forming a sort of checklist that explains how each task must be done.

2. Range – a variety of conditions, or contexts, under which the task should be carried out.

3. Knowledge and understanding – a list of things that you have to know and which are directly relevant to the task.

The next illustration shows how the performance criteria, range, knowledge and understanding work together:

A fictitious example of performance criteria, range, knowledge and understanding

*This is the **Element, the main outcome***

Help customers to make appointments for services and treatments

Deal with customer requests for **appointments** promptly and politely
Find out what the customer wants
Confirm the **appointment details** back to the customer
Make sure all the **appointment details** are correct

*The **Performance criteria** say what you have to do*

*The **Range** explains the contexts in which the task is done*

Appointments are made face to face with the customer or by phone
Appointment details record customer name, contact details, type of service, date and time

How good communication is conducted with customers
How to take messages for other people
How and when to ask questions

*The **Knowledge and understanding** tells us what we need to know*

Completing the activities

The chapters of this book cover all the essential parts of Hairdressing Level 1 NVQ and the linked activities will help you to learn what you need to know. These activities will:

- make it easier to remember important information
- help you to prepare for assessment
- provide supporting evidence and a record of your endeavours.

Not all the activities can be answered from the information in this book. Many of them will need you to search for the answers in other sources. This kind of 'self-directed' learning will make it easier to remember the information at assessment time. As you work through this book, try to get into the habit of writing down important words. At the end of each chapter, summarise the key facts and make a record of all the situations in which these topics occurred in your workplace. Some activities will need to be countersigned by a supervisor in your workplace – make a point of obtaining signatures as you work through the activities, so that the dates are correct.

Under assessment

Competence, or your ability to carry out a task to standard, is measured during assessment. Your ability to carry out the task, i.e. performance evidence, will be observed and measured against the performance criteria. So your assessor will be watching to see how you carry out your work. Sometimes, when it's not possible to cover all the situations that might crop up, your assessor might ask you questions about what you have done and how you might behave in different situations. To help you get used to this, the activities sections contain lots of the type of question that you might be asked.

Your understanding and background knowledge of work tasks are also assessed by question-and-answer techniques. Sometimes you might be asked to give a personal account of what you have learned. This could take the form of writing a sequence of events that need to be done, for example to complete a task satisfactorily. In other questioning situations you might be asked specific questions about particular tasks; more often than not, these types of question take the form of short-answer questions. Again, the activities in this book give plenty of examples and practice.

Health and safety

2

Introduction

Health and safety laws are designed to protect both you and your clients. So your personal health and hygiene, and safe methods of work, are absolutely essential. This chapter covers everything you need to know about health and safety. For your assessment, you will need to show that you can:

- recognise potential hazards and reduce their risk to health and safety
- work carefully, being aware of your workspace and of those who share it
- take personal responsibility for your own health, hygiene and presentation at work.

The NVQ Health and Safety unit is relevant for everyone at work and comprises two mandatory elements:

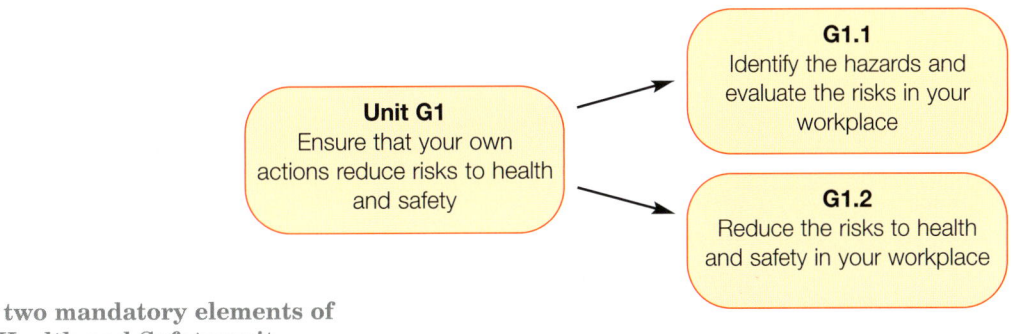

The two mandatory elements of the Health and Safety unit

Begin Hairdressing

Remember

The Health and Safety at Work Act (1974) is the 'overall' or 'umbrella' legislation, under which all other regulations are made:

- Employers have a legal duty and responsibility to ensure the health, safety and welfare of the people within the workplace.
- All people at work have a duty and responsibility not to harm themselves or others through the work they do.

Key words

Hazard is something with potential to cause harm.

Risk is the likelihood of the hazard's potential being realised.

The Health and Safety at Work Act (1974)

The aims of the Health and Safety at Work Act (1974) (HASAWA) are to:

- secure the health, safety and welfare of people while they work
- protect the health and safety of others from risks that arise from the activities of people at work.

The HASAWA is relevant to people on work experience, people who are employed or self-employed and people who work on a contracted basis.

What do you need to know?

In element G1.1 Identify the Hazards and Evaluate the Risks in your Workplace you should:

- show that you understand the health and safety requirements and policies of your workplace
- check and be aware of your own working routines and work areas, so that you can minimise the risk that you or anyone else is harmed
- be able to identify the risk arising from any hazards, know which risks you can deal with safely and identify those risks that should be reported to senior team members.

In element G1.2 Reduce the Risks to Health and Safety in your Workplace you should:

- show that you can spot potential hazards and take steps to reduce risks to the health and safety of those that might be affected within the workplace
- be able to carry out tasks safely and in line with the workplace policy and your employer's instructions.

Health and safety

Now try these out!

The Health and Safety at Work Act (1974) covers many smaller component regulations.

Activity

See if you can match the legal regulations on the left with the appropriate health and safety issues on the right (tip: look at the wording of the regulations – this will help you work out the appropriate links).

Regulations	Health and Safety Issues
Workplace (Health, Safety & Welfare) Regulations (1992)	Always wear gloves and aprons when handling chemical compounds
Manual Handling Operations Regulations (1992)	Correct and safe operation of salon equipment
Provision and Use of Work Equipment Regulations (1992)	Salon chemical products must be stored and kept safely at all times
Personal Protective Equipment at Work Regulations (1992)	Dermatitis a notifiable skin condition that results from sensitivity to chemicals
Control of Substances Hazardous to Health Regulations (1992) (COSHH)	Monitoring and maintenance of workplace hygiene and cleanliness
Electricity at Work Regulations (1989)	Always keep well stocked, just in case of accidents occuring at work
Reporting of Injuries, Diseases & Dangerous Occurences Regulations (1985)	Manufacturer information relating to the use of chemical products
Cosmetic Products (Safety) Regulations (1989)	The movement and handling of objects needs to be done safely and properly
Health & Safety (First Aid) Regulations (1981)	Items of salon electrical equipment must be checked and tested each year

Activity

Find out the following information from your work experience provider or placement then complete the details in the space provided.

Q1 Who has overall responsibility for health and safety?
A1 Name:.................................

Q2 What is this person's role in the work place?
A2 Job role:................................

Q3 If you found something that you felt was not safe at work, who would you report it to?
A3 Name:.................................

Q4 What sort of unsafe things do you think you might find? (List as many as you can)
A4 ....
   ....
   ....

Q5 In relation to product use; why are the manufacturer's instructions important?
A5 ....

Q6 What is the salon's policy in respect to maintaining a healthy and safe work environment?
A6 ....

Supervisor's signature:............. **Date:**...........

Activity

Now try these example questions and model assessment answers.

Q1 Why are you responsible for your own actions regarding health and safety at work?
A1 I need to take care in the way that I carry out my work, so that I don't have any accidents.

Q2 Why do you have to look out for others at work?
A2 The things I do at work could have a direct effect on the health and safety of others in the workplace.

Health and safety 11

 Activity

Look at the organisational diagram and answer the questions.

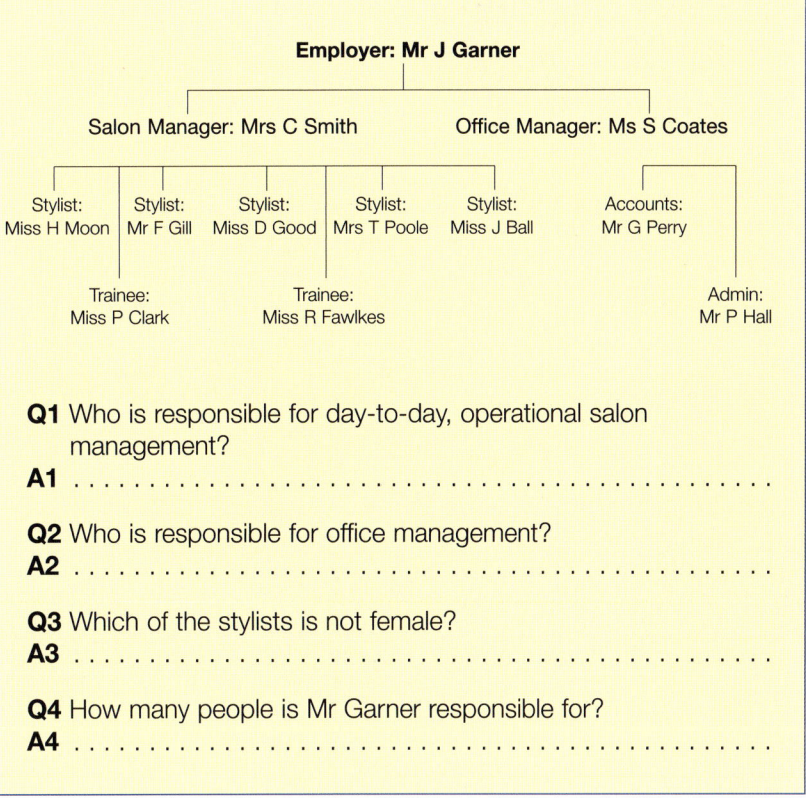

Employer: Mr J Garner

Salon Manager: Mrs C Smith   Office Manager: Ms S Coates

Stylist: Miss H Moon | Stylist: Mr F Gill | Stylist: Miss D Good | Stylist: Mrs T Poole | Stylist: Miss J Ball | Accounts: Mr G Perry

Trainee: Miss P Clark   Trainee: Miss R Fawlkes   Admin: Mr P Hall

Q1 Who is responsible for day-to-day, operational salon management?
A1 ....

Q2 Who is responsible for office management?
A2 ....

Q3 Which of the stylists is not female?
A3 ....

Q4 How many people is Mr Garner responsible for?
A4 ....

 Activity

Now complete your own organisational workplace chart.

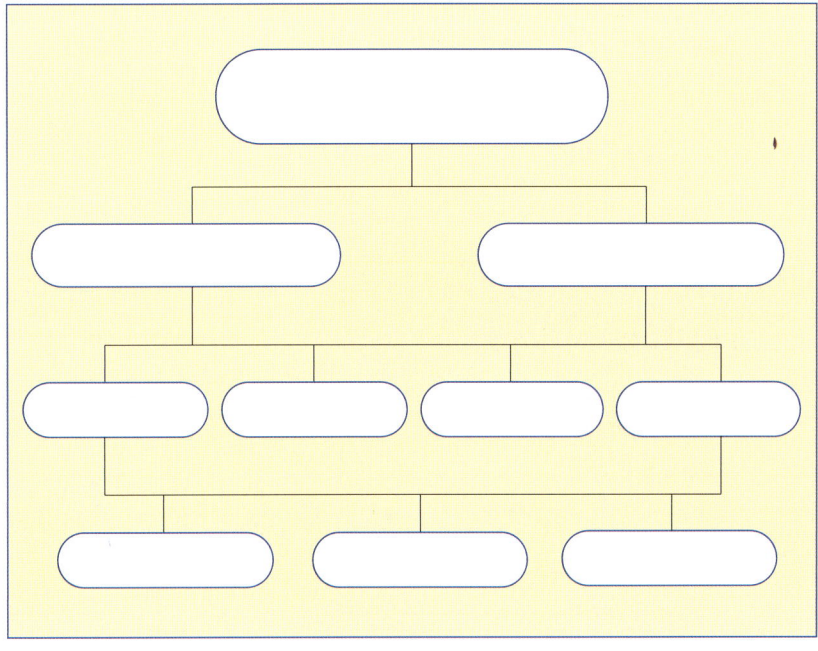

Hazard and risk

Almost anything can be a hazard but it needn't become a risk. You share a responsibility with your work colleagues for the safety of everyone within the salon (clients and colleagues), so you need to be aware of the types of hazard that can exist.

Hazards of the environment

- Wet or slippery floors.
- Cluttered passageways or corridors.
- Light bulbs that don't work.
- Trailing leads or flexes.
- Worn carpet or damaged floorings.

Hazards to do with equipment and materials

- Worn or faulty electrical equipment.
- Incorrectly labelled cleaning fluids or salon chemicals.
- Leaking or damaged containers.

Hazards to do with people

- Visitors to the salon.
- Handling things (stock, furniture, maintenance).
- Intruders.

Lawrain Aumonier of David Aumonier

Health and safety

Remember

Being aware of potential hazards is not enough, you can help minimise risks by taking prompt action.

Reporting hazards

Tell the appropriate person immediately if the degree of hazard is beyond your own responsibility (see also the Appendix: Health And Safety Regulations). For example:

- Faulty equipment:
    damaged or worn flexes
    loose plugs/electrical contacts
    damaged or broken items – tongs, dryers, straightening irons, etc.
- Loose or damaged fittings:
    mirrors, shelving, chairs, basins, etc.
- Obstructions:
    heavy items that cannot be safely moved on your own.

Dealing with hazards

If you can deal directly with the hazard you have taken personal responsibility for solving the problem:

Trailing flexes	Roll them up tidily and store them safely
Cluttered doorways and corridors	Remove the objects and store them safely or dispose of them properly
Fire or smoke	Raise the alarm and follow the emergency evacuation procedures

Risk assessment

This is the process of assessing and documenting all hazards within the work environment. Every salon must produce a detailed risk assessment report on the specific hazards relating to that particular salon.

Remember

You can check for hazards:

Floors
Are they slippery or wet?

Doorways
Are they clear of obstacles?

Electrical flexes
Are they loose or trailing?

Chemical products
Are they labelled and stored correctly?

Equipment items
Are they worn or in need of immediate attention?

Simon Shaw for WAHL

Java for Hair

Now try these out!

Hazards and risks: the left-hand list contains a number of hazards that you might find in the salon.

Activity

Write down the risk that might occur if each hazard is left unattended.

Hazard	Risk
Cups, plates and cutlery left out unwashed over a weekend	....
Kitchen bleach spilt onto the work surfaces	....
Boxes of stock left out in reception	....
Hairstyling tools not cleaned regularly after use	....

The column on the left lists some items of personal protective equipment (PPE) that are commonly available in all salons.

Activity

Write in the space provided when and why they are used.

PPE	When is it used?	Why is it used?
Disposable latex gloves	....	....
Gowns and towels	....	....
Stylist's waterproof apron	....	....
Barrier cream	....	....
Cotton wool	....	....

16 Begin Hairdressing

Activity

Now fill in the following example questions and model assessment answers.

Q1 Who has overall responsibility for your health and safety at work?
A1 .... has overall responsibility.

Q2 Who is directly responsible for your health and safety at work?
A2 .... is the person I should take up any health and safety issues that I have on a day-to-day basis.

Q3 What hazards might exist in the salon you work in?
Q ....
....
....
(*You should be able to list anything specific to the salon you work in.*)

Q4 If you found a hazard that you could not put right yourself, who would you report it to?
A4 ....
.... (probably the same person as A2, above).

Supervisor's signature: .... **Date:** ....

Activity

Do it or report it? Write the action you should take in the appropriate column.

Hazard	Sort it out myself		Report it	
Unsafe stacking of boxes in the stock room	Yes	No	Yes	No
Faulty kettle in the kitchen	Yes	No	Yes	No
Failed light bulb in the corridor	Yes	No	Yes	No
Spillage on the salon floor	Yes	No	Yes	No
A broken glass in the kitchen	Yes	No	Yes	No
Smoke appearing around the door of a closed room	Yes	No	Yes	No
Bare cable showing on the flex of a hand dryer	Yes	No	Yes	No

Supervisor's signature: .... **Date:** ....

Remember

If you are not sure ask someone

A safe working environment

Toni & Guy

You play an important part in spotting potential hazards and preventing accidents; you therefore help to avoid an emergency situation arising.

So how can you make a difference?

Suppose, for example, that someone had blocked a fire door with some recently delivered stock. You could take the initiative and move the box to a safe and secure location.

If you notice a potential hazard that you cannot easily rectify yourself, tell your supervisor immediately. Imagine, for instance, that someone accidentally tripped over a trailing lead from a hand dryer while it was plugged in, wrenching the lead from the dryer handle on to a wet floor!

Obstructions

Obstructed walkways are dangerous, regardless of whether the obstruction is in a doorway or a corridor, on stairs or on a fire exit. In an emergency, people might have to leave the salon in a hurry – perhaps even in the dark if the electricity has been cut off. It could be disastrous if someone injured themselves or fell.

So always be on the lookout for any obstruction in these areas. If you see something that could present a risk, move it away as quickly as you can.

Remember

- Always wear the gloves provided by the salon for clearing up spilled chemicals or cleaning products. Never attempt to do it without them.

- Special note: salon stylists tend to use disposable latex gloves in their work as these are more hygienic and provide better sensitivity when working on clients.

Spillage and breakages

Stop and think. You need to act quickly!

- First of all, what has been spilled or dropped? Do you know what it is?
- Is this something that needs special care and attention when handling?
- Should you report the situation to someone else or can you handle the situation yourself?
- If you are going to deal with it, should you be wearing gloves?
- What else do you need to do to rectify the situation safely without creating another hazard?

Begin Hairdressing

Now try these out!

Activity

Your salon's policy health and safety policy: find out the answers to the following questions.

> Q1 What would be considered as safe working practice at your salon?
> A1 ....
>
> Q2a Where is the salon's first aid box?
> A2a ....
>
> Q2b What items are kept in it?
> A2b ....
>
> Q3 What are the salon rules regarding smoking and consuming food and drink on the premises. And what is the policy on alcohol and other drugs?
> A3 ....
>
> Q4 What are the salon's emergency evacuation procedures?
> A4 ....
>
> Q5 What are the salon's expectations in respect to your personal presentation and hygiene?
> A5 ....
>
> **Supervisor's signature:** .... **Date:** ....

Activity

Find it and fill in how substances can be hazardous.

> Q1a What type of container is liquid or creme hydrogen peroxide kept in?
> A1a ....
>
> Q1b Why is hydrogen peroxide hazardous to health?
> A1b ....
>
> Q2a Permanent hair dyes (tints) are packaged in?
> A2a ....
>
> Q2b What chemicals are found in permanent hair dyes?
> A2b ....
>
> Q3a How should hair bleaching powder be stored?
> A3a ....
>
> Q3b Why is hair bleaching powder hazardous to health?
> A3b ....
>
> Q4a How are shampoos and conditioners stored ready for use at the backwash?
> A4a ....
>
> Q4b How are they dispensed when they are used on clients?
> A4b ....
>
> Q5a What type of container is perm solution kept in?
> A5a ....
>
> Q5b What hazard to health does perm solution present?
> A5b ....

Toni & Guy

Health and safety

Activity

In what ways can substances be hazardous to health?

Contact	With the surface of the skin or eyes
Absorption?	....
Inhalation?	....
Ingestion?	....

Activity

You are asked to mix up a permanent hair colour for a stylist.

Q1 In what way are different permanent hair colourants identified?
A1 Each different shade has a special number and a shade name.

Q2 How much product do you use?
A2 The stylist would tell me how much is needed.

Q3 How much developer would you mix with the colour product?
A3 The manufacturer's information tells you the proportions to mix.

Q4 Why is it important to follow the manufacturer's instructions?
A4 It would be easy to get the proportions wrong, which could mean that the product does not work properly or actually becomes dangerous.

Although hairdressing products are not generally thought to be hazardous, they do contain substances covered by the Control of Substances Hazardous to Health (COSHH) regulations. Your salon will have a copy of the booklet A Guide to Health & Safety of Salon Hair Products.

Preventing infection

It might be an obvious thing to say but it is essential that the salon does not become a public health hazard. For example, head lice – which are common in school children – will spread quickly in the warmth and humidity of the salon. Equally, if bacteria can find food in the form of dust and dirt, they can reproduce rapidly (for more information, see Chapter 5).

Health and Safety Law

What you should know

HSE
Health & Safety Executive

Did you know that: head lice

S Lewis

This extremely common infestation can be very difficult to eradicate. Particularly 'popular' among school children, head lice are minute animal parasites. The infection can be observed in either the egg stage or the 'adult' head louse stage, depending on how long the client has been infected.

BLM Health

Head lice are passed from person-to-person through direct contact and infestation is always accompanied by itching (caused by the parasite biting the scalp to feed on the host's blood). The adult louse lays eggs (called nits) and 'cements' these to individual hairs close to the scalp. The incubation period is short and within days an immature louse emerges.

A number of products to combat head lice can be obtained from the chemist or, alternatively, from natural remedy sources and herbalists. Getting rid of the animal parasite is fairly easy but it is much more difficult to eradicate the nits. After an infected person has been treated with the shampoo or lotion, the nits need to be removed to break the head louse life cycle.

The easiest way to remove the nits is to use a fine-tooth nit-comb when the hair is still wet. Applying vinegar (a mild acid solution) to the hair tightens the hair cuticle layer and makes it easier to comb away the nits. A final shampoo will remove any unpleasant smell and the hair is free from infestation.

Personal health, hygiene and appearance

Hairdressing, beauty therapy and nail craft are personal services and as such are very different to trades such as retail, joinery or engineering in the way that they communicate to and handle their clients. Salon staff and their clients can have quite a close relationship, which has its advantages and disadvantages. Your clients will judge your personal and professional standards by the ways in which you present yourself and communicate.

Hands and nails

Your hands should always be perfectly clean. Dirt on your hands and under your nails will harbour bacteria and if you spread germs you could infect other people. Your hands need to washed not only before you go to work but several times during the day. When you are shampooing and conditioning, your hands could lose moisture and become dry and cracked. Broken skin allows germs to enter and infection can follow. To prevent this from happening, you should use a barrier cream. These creams cover the skin with an invisible barrier

Remember

Hairdressing is an image-conscious industry, would you give clients confidence if you turned up for appointments with stained overalls, unkempt hair and dirty hands and finger nails?

Remember

Always wear gloves:

- **When** on any occasion where you come into contact with chemicals
- **Why** because gloves are a protective barrier against infection

Always wash hands:

- **When** before work, after eating, using the toilet, and after coughing, sneezing or blowing your nose
- **Why** because your hands are one of the main sources for spreading infection

Always wear protective clothing/equipment:

- **When** always wear a plastic apron for any salon procedure involving chemicals
- **Why** this will prevent spillages onto your clothes, particularly when tinting and perming

that greatly reduces the penetration of hairdressing washing and conditioning agents. (Many trainees give up hairdressing after developing the skin condition called dermatitis, in which the hands become sore, cracked, itchy and red.)

Now try these out!

Activity

Think about how visitors and clients are treated in the salon.

> Observe the different ways customers are handled in the salon. Write your notes in the space provided below.
>
> ....
> ....
> ....
> ....
> ....
> ....
> ....
> ....
> ....
> ....
> ....

The next activity will help you to summarise some key points.

Activity

Fill in the blank spaces (the answers are all in the text above).

> What are head lice?
>
> ....
>
> An infectious condition can
>
> ....
>
> A warm, humid and poorly ventilated salon will
>
> ....
>
> Why is it important to moisturise your skin after shampooing and conditioning?
>
> ....
>
> Hairdressing, beauty therapy and nail craft are all different examples of
>
> ....

Health and safety

Many of the following conditions will be new to you.

Activity

Find out which column they belong in.

Condition	Viral disease	Bacterial infection	Fungal infection	Animal infestation
Aids				
Scalp ringworm				
Influenza				
Herpes				
Head lice				
Impetigo				
Scabies				
Athlete's foot				
Sore throat				
Dandruff				
Acne				

Activity

Now try the following example questions and model assessment answers.

Q1 Why is your personal presentation important at work?
A1 Clients will make a swift judgement on the way I present myself. The overall professionalism of the salon is a team contribution and I would not let the side down.

Q2 How might cross-infection from you to a customer occur?
A2 I could pass an infection or disease to a customer if I didn't wash my hands after going to the lavatory.

Q3 When and why would you use a barrier cream?
A3 I would use barrier cream to protect my hands from the drying effects of shampooing and conditioning.

Your body

Human skin contains sweat glands that secrete excess moisture in the form of sweat. The skin in the armpits, feet and genital area have more sweat glands than elsewhere and the warm, moist conditions in these areas provide an ideal breeding ground for bacteria. Decaying bacteria causes body odour (BO), so it is essential to take a shower/bath daily to remove the build-up of sweat, dead skin cells and surface bacteria.

Your mouth

Unpleasant breath (halitosis) can be offensive and can result from digestive disorders, stomach upsets, smoking and strong foods (e.g. onions, garlic and some cheeses) and when particles of food begin to decay in the spaces between the teeth. Frequent tooth brushing will eliminate bad breath and helps to maintain good oral hygiene.

Toni & Guy

Personal appearance

Your personal appearance is as important as your personal cleanliness. The effort you put into getting ready for work reflects your pride in the job. Your own individual look is OK, as long as you appreciate and accept that professional standards of dress and appearance must be followed.

Clothes

It's far easier to wear a uniform at work than your own clothes. They tend to be easy to clean and maintain; they also get rid of those difficult 'what to wear' choices.

If you do wear your own clothes they should be clean, well ironed and made from fabrics that are suitable not only for your intended work, but also for the time of year. Less restrictive or tight clothes will allow air to circulate around your body and will keep you cool and fresh; avoiding uncomfortable perspiration or possibly BO. Also, clothes revealing too much of your body could be considered unprofessional and possibly provocative!

Health and safety

Shoes

Hairdressing involves a lot of standing and your feet can get tired, hot, sweaty and even sore. So wear smart, comfortable shoes with low heels. It is better to wear shoes that allow your feet to 'breathe' because ventilated feet stay cool and comfortable throughout the working day. Trainers are great but check that they're OK before turning up to work in them.

Hair

When working in a salon, it is important to maintain a professional appearance and your hair needs to be clean and well presented. Long hair should be kept away from your face to allow eye contact with clients and display positive body language.

Jewellery

It is best not to wear too much jewellery because as well as harbouring germs, items such as rings and long necklaces can get in the way of everyday tasks such as washing hair. Jewellery will also cause discomfort to clients if it gets caught in hair.

Posture

Adopting the correct posture at work is essential, as bad posture leads to aches, pains or even long-term skeletal injury. An incorrect standing position will put undue strain on your back, shoulders and neck muscles and possibly the ligaments in between the joints too!

As we have already said, hairdressing involves a lot of standing and this may come as rather a shock to new recruits as a busy stylist can be on their feet for up to 6 or 7 hours a day. If you watch a stylist cutting their client's hair you will see that they need to hold the hair in many different ways, often bending their bodies and lifting their arms to achieve the precise cutting positions.

Professional posture is derived from standing correctly. Their shoulders are level, head upright and their body weight is distributed evenly over legs with feet that are

Did you know that:

Antiperspirants reduce underarm sweating. They contain astringents, which narrow the pores that release sweat and cool down the skin.

Deodorants do not reduce the amount of sweating but can mask any odour by killing the surface bacteria with antiseptic ingredients.

slightly apart. Any other standing position, i.e. dropped shoulder, hips pushed forwards or sideways appears as unprofessional. Slouching is not only uncomfortable, it is dangerous and is an example of poor body language; it communicates to clients and colleagues an uncaring attitude.

Beiersdorf UK

Now try these out!

 **Activity**

Match the information on the left with the relative statements on the right.

Regular washing		Occurs when food particles are left between teeth
Bad breath (halitosis)		Catch on the client's scalp and hair
Personal cleanliness and appearance		Can lead to fatigue or longer-term injury
Bracelets, necklaces and rings		Will prevent build-up of sweat and BO
Bad posture		Reflects your pride in your work

Health and safety

Activity

Now find out the expected standards at your place of work in relation to the following aspects.

	Standard
Your personal hygiene	....
Your jewellery	....
Your work shoes	....
Your work clothing	....

Activity

What is the company policy if you fail to meet these standards?

What is your company's policy if you fail to meet the standards above?

....
....
....
....
....
....
....
....
....

Activity

Now try the following example questions and model assessment answers.

Q1 How do you prevent BO?
A1 By taking daily showers/baths

Q2 Why is your choice of footwear important at work?
A2 Comfortable shoes are essential for hairdressing because you are on your feet most of the time.

Q3 Why is a uniform a good idea for salon work wear?
A3 Uniforms tend to be easy to clean and to look after. They eliminate having to choose what to wear and they avoid competition between staff. They give a professional team look for the salon.

Emergencies

Fire

All places of work must have adequate fighting fire equipment and means of escape. All fire exits have to be clearly marked with the appropriate signs and it must be possible to open all doors easily and immediately from the inside.

The most likely reasons for fire occurring in a hairdressing salon is from electrical fault, gas escape or the people within it:

- Faulty or badly maintained electrical equipment, such as items of salon hand equipment, and kitchen appliances, i.e. kettles, washing machines and tumble dryers, could malfunction, overheat and even ignite!
- Gas appliances, such as ovens or hobs, present a possible risk if they are left unattended.
- Overloading an electrical circuit, the positioning of unattended portable heaters and smoking can also cause fires.

Your salon will have set fire safety procedures, which must always be followed.

Raising the alarm

In the event of a fire breaking out, your main priorities are to:

- First: raise the alarm and evacuate the premises – staff and clients must be warned and the premises must be evacuated quickly and safely. Everyone should go to the designated assembly point.
- Second: call the Fire Brigade. Do this even if you believe that someone else has already phoned. Dial 999, ask the operator for the Fire Service and give the telephone number from where you are calling. Wait for the transfer to the Fire Service then tell them your name and the address of the premises that are on fire.

Remember

Fire fighting

Only people who have been trained should attempt to fight a fire. **Under no circumstance should you attempt to fight the fire yourself.**

Accidents (first aid)

Most accidents in a hairdressing salon will be the result of handling sharp equipment (e.g. scissors) and chemicals. By law, the employer has to provide adequate first aid equipment. A first aid box should always be kept well stocked with the following items:

The contents of a first aid box

Number of employees	1–5	6–10	11–50
First aid guidance notes	1	1	1
Individual sterile adhesive dressings	20	20	40
Sterile eye pads	1	2	4
Sterile triangular bandages	1	2	4
Safety pins	6	6	12
Medium-sized sterile unmedicated dressings	3	6	8
Large-sized sterile unmedicated dressings	1	2	4
Extra-large-sized sterile unmedicated dressings	1	2	4

Note: any first aid materials used from the kit must be replaced.

Recording accidents and illness

All accidents must be recorded in the salon's accident book. This provides a permanent record for the following details:

- date, time and place of incident or treatment
- name and job of the injured or ill person
- details of the injury or of the ill person, and of the treatment given
- what happened to the person immediately afterwards (e.g. went home, hospital)
- name and signature of the person providing the treatment and writing the entry.

Now try these out!

Activity

Types of fire extinguisher: find out which one goes with which.

- Foam
- Carbon dioxide
- Dry powder

- Red with a blue label
- Red with a cream label
- Red with a black label

Activity

Classes of fire: find out which one goes with which.

- Class A fires
- Class B fires
- Class C fires
- Class D fires

- Involves metals
- Involves liquids, e.g. petrol
- Involves solids, e.g. wood, paper
- Involves gases, e.g. propane

Activity

Now find this out!

Your workplace will have its own fire and accident procedures:

Q1 Where is this information is displayed?
A1 ....

Q2 What is the fire drill procedure?
A2 ....

Q3 Where is the accident book kept?
A3 ....

Activity

Now try this fire knowledge quiz.

Fire knowledge quiz

Q1 What is the main colour of a fire exit sign?
- ❏ green
- ❏ blue
- ❏ red
- ❏ yellow

Q2 What should you do first when you hear a fire alarm?
- ❏ phone the Fire Brigade
- ❏ evacuate the building
- ❏ check to see where the fire is
- ❏ wait in the staff room

Q3 What colour are fire extinguishers?
- ❏ red
- ❏ green
- ❏ black
- ❏ blue

Q4 Water-filled extinguishers can be used on electrical fires:
- ❏ true
- ❏ false

Q5 Fire exits must always be kept locked:
- ❏ true
- ❏ false

See the Appendix at the end of the book for a brief description of the Health and Safety legislation relating to hairdressing. Then rate yourself on the heath and safety checkerboard:

Activity

Finally, rate yourself on the checkerboard.

I understand my job position and the impact of health and safety responsibilities associated with it ☐	I know who is responsible for health and safety and who to report to, any hazards in the workplace ☐	I always follow the salon's policy in respect to health and safety practices and procedures ☐	I can recognise the hazards and potential risks at work, and take appropriate action ☐
I know what the main areas of potential risk for health and safety at work ☐	I understand all of the relevant health and safety regulations applicable to work ☐	I always carry out working practices according to the salon's policy ☐	I know why it is important to be aware of potential risks to personal health and safety ☐
I understand the implications of poor salon hygiene and cross-infecting others ☐	I can handle, use and work with: materials, products and equipment safely ☐	I understand the necessity of personal hygiene and presentation ☐	I know the salon's policy and procedures in the event of fire or accidents ☐
I know what would be considered to be unsafe practices at work ☐			**CHECKER BOARD** ✓

Receiving clients and making appointments

Introduction

The reception area is the focal point of the salon. How the person working in the reception area communicates with clients and passes information to colleagues is crucial for the overall success of the business. You play an important and vital role in that ongoing success. When you are working in the receptions area you will need to show that you can:

- keep the area neat and tidy
- greet people entering the salon and deal with their enquiries
- make appointments for clients, both face to face and by telephone.

The NVQ Level 1 unit Assist With Salon Reception Duties has three mandatory elements:

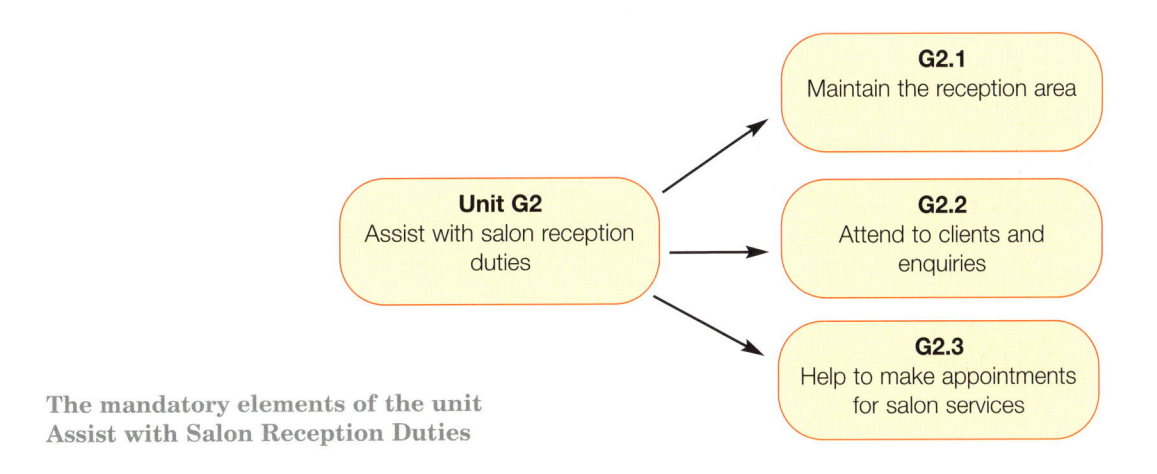

Unit G2 Assist with salon reception duties

- **G2.1** Maintain the reception area
- **G2.2** Attend to clients and enquiries
- **G2.3** Help to make appointments for salon services

The mandatory elements of the unit Assist with Salon Reception Duties

Lots of people come into the salon for many different reasons. It is important that all staff are helpful; making visitors feel welcome by giving the right impression, being able to provide accurate information and making appointments.

What do you need to know?

In element G2.1 Maintain the Reception Area you should:

- know how you keep the reception and retail areas clean and tidy
- demonstrate how to check and report on condition of stock and stationery levels
- be able to follow the customer care policy of the salon.

In element G2.2 Attend to Clients and Enquiries you should:

- demonstrate how to communicate positively
- be able to take accurate messages and pass them on reliably
- show how to handle information professionally and confidentially.

In element G2.3 Help to Make Appointments for Salon Services you should:

- discuss the services and treatments available to clients
- be able to handle the salon appointment system.

Marianne Marjerus Hairdressers Journal

Mahogany

Aa Key words

The salon **appointment system** is the efficient way of organising the work for salon operatives.

Customer care is the professional way in which customers of the salon, i.e. the clients, are looked after and their needs attended to.

Effective communication is the process by which information and messages are handled professionally.

Confidentiality is the secure way of handling personal information, ensuring only those who are permitted have access to it.

Receiving clients and making appointments

Now try these out!

The reception area is the hub of the salon: clients arrive, calls are received, visitors arrive, bills are paid and appointments are made.

Activity

Match the operations to the tasks.

Operations	Tasks
Retail products should be dusted daily	Because handling information correctly is so important
Hairstyle books and magazines are useful	Because people don't buy or handle dirty items
Offer clients a drink or magazines	Because we must convey a professional image and service
Appointments books are essential	Because they help people describe a new look
Good communication is essential	Because sometimes they have to wait for a while
Messages should always be passed on to the right person	Because they organise the stylist's day

Watch how the people in the reception area deal with clients and enquiries. What do you notice about the way they do it?

Activity

Think about how visitors and clients are treated in the salon.

How do people working in the reception area deal with clients and enquiries?

....
....
....
....
....
....
....
....
....
....
....

Activity

Now think about answering the telephone.

> What are you supposed to say when you answer the telephone?

Maintaining reception and retail areas

Remember

Even if our communication skills are perfect, what clients see around them has a far greater impact on their arrival than anything we have to say.

Hairdressing is a personal service industry and if we are going to keep our clients happy, we have to provide a complete and professional service. This service is not just focused around the stylist's abilities – cutting, styling, perming or colouring – it has to have a far wider application than that.

The total service experienced by salon clients involves all the people in the salon. It is both what is done in the salon and how it is done, and you play a vital role. First impressions are lasting, and the first impression clients get is when they arrive at reception. It doesn't matter whether a visitor is new to the salon or a long-standing, regular client, the overall impression, i.e. image, of the salon is created by what they see and hear.

Now try these out!

Activity

Think about customer service and customer care.

> What is the difference between customer service and customer care?
>
> Customer service is:
>
> Customer care is:

Receiving clients and making appointments 37

Sean Hanna

Activity

Find out your salon's procedure for making appointments.

List the steps that you should take to make an appointment. Ask your supervisor to check your responses.

1 ....
....
....
2 ....
....
....
3 ....
....
....

Supervisor's signature: .... **Date:** ....

Activity

Now try these example questions and model answers.

When clients arrive at the salon for their appointment:

Q1 What's the first thing you should do when a client arrives?
A1 Check the client's name, appointment time, what they are having done and who it is with.

Q2 What should you do next?
A2 Take their coat and any shopping, etc. and put them away carefully and safely.

Q3 The stylist is not quite ready. What should you do next?
A3 Ask the client to take a seat. Offer a drink and something to look at for the time being.

Receiving clients and making appointments

> **?** **Do you know that: first impressions are lasting impressions?**
>
> The human brain can take in a wide variety of information, from different channels at the same time. How is that? We are aware of our surroundings by using any number of the five senses: sight, hearing, smell, touch and taste. These senses analyse and interpret the information we receive, helping us to create an overall impression, whether right or wrong!
>
> We process the information so quickly that we are trying to create a judgement or understanding for what we see. Generally speaking, our first and lasting impression is created in less than 10 seconds! So you don't get a second chance to create a good first impression.

> **Remember**
>
> Always confirm back to the client, the appointment details: date, time, service, name and who it is with.

Salon tidiness is essential and maintenance in reception is equally important: a clean, attractive reception and retail display conveys a message of professionalism and pride. Add to this a warm smile, good eye contact and a friendly 'Hello, how can I help you?' and instant, good customer care takes place.

Checking products and stationery

Hairdressing businesses exist by selling services and/or products to customers at a profit. Two aspects underpin this concept: efficiency and effectiveness.

Your role in the day-to-day, routine efficiency of the salon is crucial.

Imagine this: a customer arrives at the salon and wants to make an appointment. Although you remember about professional communication, after rummaging around the (admittedly rather untidy) reception desk, you can't find a pen because someone has borrowed it to make out a stock list. What do you do? Do you leave the customer unattended while you go off to find another? What sort of message will that send?

Errors like this, as simple as it seems, happen all the time. But they needn't, at least, not if your mind is on the job! Always make a point of checking the reception area:

- The desk must be tidied and dusted ready for clients.

> **Remember**
>
> **Efficiency and effectiveness:**
>
> **Efficiency** refers to the way that all work runs smoothly
>
> **Effectiveness** refers to the way that the work maximises the allocation of time.

Begin Hairdressing

> **Remember**
>
> When making appointments, try to offer a range of dates at different times for the client. If a client can't make an appointment in the week around 3.30 pm she may be at work, so offering another day at the same time will probably be unsuitable too.

- The appointment diary should be close to hand and ready for use.
- There should be sufficient stationery and writing materials for changing and making appointments, taking notes or messages.

If items are missing, mislaid or in need of replacement, let someone know.

L'Oréal Professionnel

L'Oréal Professionnel

Receiving clients and making appointments

Remember

Never hurry a phone call for an appointment. Rushed call handling is poor communication, rude, and will lead to making mistakes in the booking.

A similar situation applies to retail displays too:

- Shelves should be cleaned and products dusted every day.
- Missing items and items with low stock levels should be replaced or reported.
- Damaged or faulty products should be removed from display and reported.
- Products should be rearranged and gaps in product lines removed by bringing other items closer to the shelf edge, enabling easier access.
- Product information and pricing should be relative to items, close by and easy to read.

Don't forget, if you are to provide basic information on product availability and prices to customers, you will need to have a reasonable working knowledge of the products that your salon offers.

Activity

Now try these out!

List the following retail product information from your salon.

List the following retail product information from your salon

Retail product name	What is it used for?	When is it used?	Sales price
. . . .	. . . .	. . . .	. . . .
. . . .	. . . .	. . . .	. . . .
. . . .	. . . .	. . . .	. . . .
. . . .	. . . .	. . . .	. . . .
. . . .	. . . .	. . . .	. . . .
. . . .	. . . .	. . . .	. . . .
. . . .	. . . .	. . . .	. . . .
. . . .	. . . .	. . . .	. . . .
. . . .	. . . .	. . . .	. . . .

Activity

Now think about your salon's policy for retail displays.

> **Q1** Why do the retail displays need to be kept clean and tidy?
> **A1** ....
>
> **Q2** What is the procedure in relation to damaged or leaking products?
> **A2** ....
>
> **Q3** What items of; and how much stationery needs to be kept at the reception desk?
> **A3** ....
>
> **Q4** In what circumstances or situations are you expected to ask for help?
> **A4** ....
>
> **Q5** Who would be the first person to contact if the occasion arises?
> **A5** ....
>
> **Supervisor's signature:** .... **Date:** ....

We can use our senses to create an overall impression in the same way that clients do when they arrive at the salon.

Activity

For each of the senses below, what would create a positive image and what a negative image.

Senses	Positive image	Negative image
Sight		
Hear		
Taste		
Smell	Fresh flowers at the desk	Client gowns in need of washing!
Touch		

In the exercise above we have noted that an indicator of negative image could be simply a gown that needed washing; it might have looked clean but the linger of stale perfume tells the tale!

Receiving clients and making appointments

Activity

Now think about some other aspects of the salon that might need attention.

Q1 What sort of things around the salon might you find that need immediate attention, cleaning, washing or removal?
A1 ....

Q2 What action would you take in finding them?
A2 ....

Remember

Dust the products on the retail displays regularly, no-one wants to handle products that look murky and dull, regardless of how fabulous they are.

Sean Hanna

Greeting people and dealing with their enquiries

We want visitors to become our clients and there are ways to make this happen. An important part of this process, and one that affects the conscious decisions people make about us, is communication. We want people to see us as professional communicators. Professional communication occurs when we handle or anticipate the needs of others in a prompt and 'business-like' manner. Effective communication takes place in the following ways:

- Speech – in what we say to others and the way we say it.
- Listening – by hearing the requests of others.
- Writing – by recording information accurately and clearly.
- Body language – the way we communicate our feelings and attitude to situations by posture, expression and mannerisms.

Sean Hanna

Receiving clients and making appointments

> **Remember**
>
> Never leave callers hanging on the line for more than a few seconds without checking with them first. At best, it's frustrating, at worst, they might hang up all together!

Enquiries made either in person (i.e. 'face-to-face') or on the telephone should be handled in the same way. In both instances we need to respond promptly and politely. If you don't know the answer to a question, ask someone who does – accurate information is essential. So stop! Listen to what is being said, hear the request and act on the information. Misinterpreting what has been said could result in giving or recording the wrong information. A disaster when making appointments, imagine if the client turns up on the wrong day and can't be done because her stylist is too busy!

It is even more difficult on the telephone, when callers gain an impression of the salon only from the person they are speaking to. This person becomes the salon's sole representative, acting on behalf of the business, and his or her ability to listen, speak clearly, respond to requests and act upon information is vital.

Smile when you answer the telephone – people will 'hear' the friendliness in your voice. At the same time, speak clearly so that the caller understands everything you say. After listening to the caller's request, confirm the main points back to the caller. This summarises the information and ensures that all details are correct. Keep in mind the length of the call, calls cost money and waste valuable salon time.

When clients arrive in person, they should be attended to promptly, their appointment and time should be checked before they are directed to a seat. Always make a point of making them feel welcome, perhaps offer a magazine or a drink before telling the stylist they have arrived. This is important – it will avoid any unnecessary waiting or possible embarrassment when the stylist realises (perhaps much later) that their client has actually arrived.

There will be occasions when you need to seek the assistance or advice from others. Being able to recognise situations when you are unable to help is not a failure, it is all part of professional communication. There will be situations that require the attention of someone else; the window cleaner arrives and says 'Shall I just get on with it?' or when stock arrives and the signature of a person responsible for taking delivery and accepting condition of goods is required.

The visual impressions made from a person's body language are also important. These silent gestures (non-verbal communication) convey messages to others:

- 'I'm really interested' (leaning forward on the edge of the seat, head up and hair pushed behind the ears)
- 'I'm not at all happy' (sitting right back on the sofa, head down with folded arms)
- 'I don't believe you' (an arm folded across the chest while the other arm gently strokes the chin or rub an ear lobe)
- 'It's the truth' (standing up straight with arms, waist high, palms open and facing forwards).

Chris Moody

A professional communicator can interpret a wide range of unspoken stances and inferences. And you can be a good communicator by always making sure that your own personal body language is right.

- Eye contact – this is important and should be maintained when talking to clients. When possible, your amount of eye contact should be the same or less than the client's. This shows that you are not trying to talk down to the client or to make him or her feel intimidated.

Receiving clients and making appointments

- Distances are important too – everyone has their 'comfort zone' (the immediate space that surrounds us). Getting too close and invading someone's space will immediately make that person back off and feel uncomfortable.
- It is generally accepted that people don't like to be ignored. So don't leave someone standing at reception without being acknowledged. Slouching and bad posture at reception is also a major 'put off'. People want to see eagerness and you can demonstrate your willingness to help by remaining alert.

Taking messages

Remember

Always keep a pad for notes handy at reception. It will provide a far more useful aide, than writing over the appointment page!

You will sometimes need to take a message on behalf of someone else. It is essential that these messages are recorded accurately recorded and delivered promptly to the appropriate person. Always keep a message pad close to the telephone, writing messages on the appointment book is unprofessional and must be avoided at all costs. When taking messages, always make sure that you record the time and date, and make clear who the message is for and who it is from. Then give as much detail as you can relating to the nature of the message:

- who the message for
- who has taken it
- the date and time received
- the purpose or content of the message.

Confidentiality

Certain circumstances need special care and attention and probably the most important aspect of professional communication is confidentiality. During our day-to-day work it is possible that we come into contact with information that others consider private. It is important that you recognise these situations and handle them accordingly. This confidential information will occur in numerous ways: during routine conversation between staff or clients and from business contacts and inquirers.

Whatever the source, you must not divulge personal or potentially sensitive information to anyone.

Now try these out!

Activity

In the spaces provided, log three entries for messages that you have taken at work. Then get your workplace supervisor to sign and date, to verify your examples.

Date:............ Time:....................

I agree that the message given was clear, correct passed on and fully understood.

Signed: ....

Supervisor's comments: ....
....
....
....

Activity

Now think about why taking messages and passing them on to the correct person is so important.

Taking messages and passing them on to the correct person is important because: ....
....
....
....
....
....
....

Confidentiality is another issue: during your work routine you overhear a client say to the stylist 'Yes, I've just picked up my holiday money. It's about a thousand in cash. I'm going to keep it in my bag until we go on Friday.'

Activity

Think about confidentiality.

What could happen if you inadvertently broke a client's confidentiality by telling someone unconnected with the situation what you had heard? Write your reply below:
....
....
....
....

Activity

Body language is also important. Match the mannerisms on the right with the inferences on the left.

Mannerisms	Inferences
Talking with open palms	I find it hard to believe
Inability to look someone in the eye	I'm not listening to you
Rubbing the ears or back of the neck	Honesty and truthfulness
Sat back with arms tightly folded	I'm really pushy and dominating
Moving into someones comfort zone uninvited	I'm not very confident

Making appointments

A business should operate like a 'well oiled' machine, all the components should work together smoothly without rubbing, overheating, straining or wear. At the very centre – the 'hub' of the operation – is the appointment system. Without an appointment system the business would stop! So it is essential that appointments are made accurately and promptly, every time, whether the client makes the appointment over the telephone or in person.

Before you can schedule appointments you must have an idea of the services available. Each salon offers a unique 'menu' of services. Different stylists will have different abilities and skills, and so might be available only for certain services at certain levels. Get to know exactly the variety of services, the timings and costs that the salon and its stylists have to offer.

Making appointments needn't be difficult. It's about matching client requests with the time available. We want to help the customer make the booking, while bearing in mind the time it will take and who will be providing the service. When clients are contacting the salon by telephone you should always speak first, saying 'Good morning/afternoon this is Head Masters hair salon, Hayley speaking how can I

Remember

Always introduce yourself when handling calls. People like to speak to people they can associate with, not strangers or machines!

help you?' This friendly but positive approach will immediately give a professional image of both the salon and yourself.

Each salon has its own system for making appointments but, generally speaking, appointment scheduling is completed in such a way as to maximise the time available with appropriate staff members. Bearing this in mind, we should always remain ready, prompt and polite in attending to the client's requests.

Make sure that when the booking is made that you record the information accurately and clearly and that you have considered all the factors:

- date and time
- service required
- stylist required
- the client's name
- client contact details.

Sean Hanna

Record the client's name clearly in the appointment system, alongside the service, and check that it is scheduled for the correct day and time with the appropriate stylist. As a matter of customer service it is also useful to give the client an approximate idea of service cost and length of appointment time. At the end, summarise all the information back to the client; this will ensure that all the details are correct.

If in doubt

When you are not sure, it is always better to ask someone else than to make an incorrect booking. When unsure, always ask someone else for help. There is nothing worse than a stylist running late, particularly if this is the result of someone else's booking error. This situation will be stressful for the stylist but, more importantly, we do not want clients to wait any longer than absolutely necessary, whatever the reason.

Now try these out!

Activity

List the range of services available from your salon.

Service name:	....
Which stylists provide this service:	....
What happens in this service:	....
What do they cost:	....

Activity

Next, do a self-assessment of how you handle telephone appointments.

Did you answer the phone promptly?	Yes	❏	No	❏
Did you answer the phone politely?	Yes	❏	No	❏
Did you say your name and how may I help you?	Yes	❏	No	❏
Did you accurately record the details?	Yes	❏	No	❏
Did you summarise back to the client the appointment information?	Yes	❏	No	❏

Activity

Now consider what would happen if an appointment was made incorrectly.

Q1 Who would be affected?

A1 ....

Q2 What impression would it give?

A2 ....

Q3 How would the business be affected?

A3 ....

Activity

Next, consider some service information and complete a blank appointment sheet.

A salon employs three hairstylists:

- Jane: stylist who works part-time 1 p.m. to 5.30 p.m.
- Samantha: stylist who works full-time 9 a.m. to 5.30 p.m. and has an hour for lunch
- Tina: colourist who works mornings only 9 a.m. to 12 noon

Service	Duration
Cut and blow dry (CBD)	45 minutes
Blow dry (BD)	30 minutes
Wet cut only (WC)	30 minutes
Dry trim (DT)	15 minutes
High-lights T section (HLT)	30 minutes (plus 30 minutes development)
High-lights full head (HL fh)	45 minutes (plus 30 minutes development)
Retouch colour (Col rt)	30 minutes (plus 45 minutes development)

Now read the following service information and complete the blank appointment sheet using the appropriate abbreviations:

Mrs Cooper, a regular client, has a standing appointment with Samantha for a blow dry at 10 a.m.

Miss Cooper's daughter would like full-head high-lights at the same time as her mother, with a cut and blow dry back with Samantha later.

Mrs Ford wants the earliest appointment available with Jane for a cut and blow dry and would like to bring her two children for dry trims with whoever is available at the same time.

Miss Jones would like a mid-morning cut and blow dry appointment with Samantha.

A Miss Collins rings to ask if there is an appointment to retouch her colour and then a cut and blow dry back with Samantha after 10.30 a.m.

Mark out time for Samantha's lunch.

Two college girls, Miss Green and Miss Dorkin, call in and ask if there are any appointments for cut and blow drys, after lectures and as near to 2.00 p.m. as possible. They don't mind who they have, but they would like it at the same time.

Someone rings at 1.00 p.m. and asks for their children, Paula and Cheryl Tombs, to have a wet cut and a dry trim, respectively, before 3.00 p.m. She wants to know when they can be fitted in.

Receiving clients and making appointments | 53

Date: ....

Time	Stylist	Stylist	Stylist
9.00			
9.15			
9.30			
9.45			
10.00			
10.15			
10.30			
10.45			
11.00			
11.15			
11.30			
11.45			
12.00			
12.15			
12.30			
12.45			
1.00			
1.15			
1.30			
1.45			
2.00			
2.15			
2.30			
2.45			
3.00			
3.15			
3.30			
3.45			
4.00			
4.15			
4.30			
4.45			
5.00			
5.15			
5.30	Leave	Leave	Leave

Q1 The manager has arranged for a technical demonstration for cutting and styling. This will take at least 2 hours and the stylists will need to tidy around first. What time can this training session start?
(mark it on the appointment sheet as DEMO).
A1 ....

Q2 What time will the training session finish?
A2 ....

Q3 Samantha and Tina both did a full stock check and reorder. They spent 45 minutes together. When did they do it?
(mark this on the appointment sheet as Stock control).
A3 ....

Begin Hairdressing

Activity

Finally, rate yourself on the checkerboard.

I understand my job and the impact of not keeping information confidential ☐	I know how to record accurate information for messages and appointments ☐	I always follow the salon's policy in respect to client care and customer service ☐	I know who I can turn to if I have any difficulties at work ☐
I know who to turn to for help with reception duties ☐	I understand the extent to which Data Protection Act affects what I do at work ☐	I always carry out working practices according to the salon's policy ☐	I know how to communicate effectively with staff and customers ☐
I understand the implications of poor client communications ☐	I know how to say things in different ways in order to be tactful and courteous ☐	I understand the necessity of personal presentation when dealing with clients ☐	I know the salon's services; how long they take and how much they cost ☐
I know what to look for in relation to stationery shortages and product imperfections ☐			**CHECKER BOARD** ✓

Working together

4

Introduction

The relationships that must be built and maintained at work are very different to those that exist outside the working environment. A hairdressing business relies on providing repeated services to customers at a profitable price that they are prepared to pay. This formula might seem simple, but it isn't, and a great many factors affect this delicate balance. Unfortunately, unlike other businesses, personal service relies solely on people and the communications between them. It has very little to do with selling a commodity (i.e. a product).

So what's the difference? Well, in selling a product, more often than not, the purchaser has made a conscious decision to buy. The standard or quality is defined by the product's composition. The only factors affecting the sale are competing products and their price, availability features and benefits.

In hairdressing, the standard and quality of hairdressing skills provided by stylists of the same level of expertise might vary only slightly between salons. So another, far more important, variable, comes into play: what matters is not so much what is provided but how it is provided. Thus communication becomes the vital link, not to sell products, but to sell a complete service.

The relationship that must be built and maintained between you, your colleagues and your clients is the key factor in making hairdressing a success. You will need to show that you can:

- create a good impression with clients
- create good working relationships with staff
- build on your abilities at work.

The unit Contribute to the Development of Effective Working Relationships comprises three mandatory elements:

Unit G3 Contribute to the development of effective working relationships

- **G3.1** Develop effective working relationships with clients
- **G3.2** Develop effective working relationships with colleagues
- **G3.3** Develop yourself within the job role

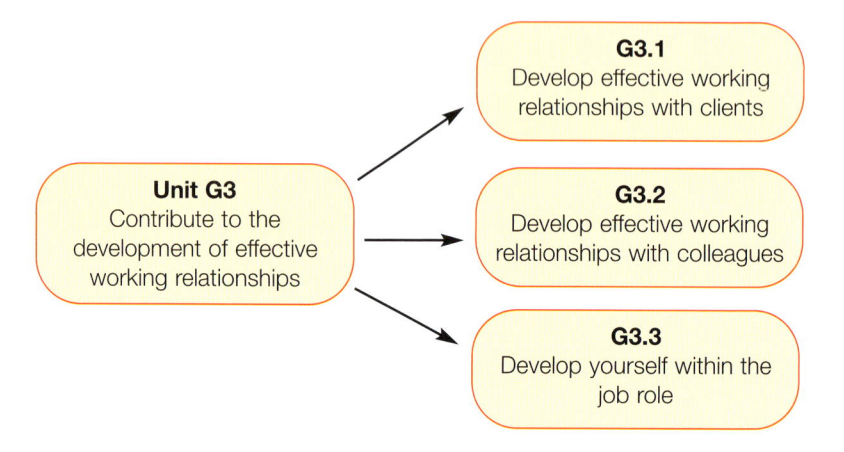

The three mandatory elements of the unit Contribute to the Development of Effective Working Relationships

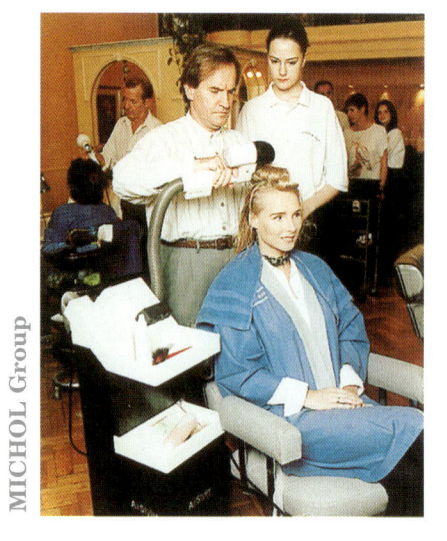

What do you need to know?

In element G3.1 Develop Effective Working Relationships with Clients you should:

- show that can communicate in a clear, polite and confident way
- demonstrate your knowledge and understanding of the principles of professional communication
- be able to promote goodwill and trust.

In element G3.2 Develop Effective Working Relationships with Colleagues you should:

- demonstrate your knowledge and understanding of the differences between work and non-work relationships
- be able to assist others in their work roles.

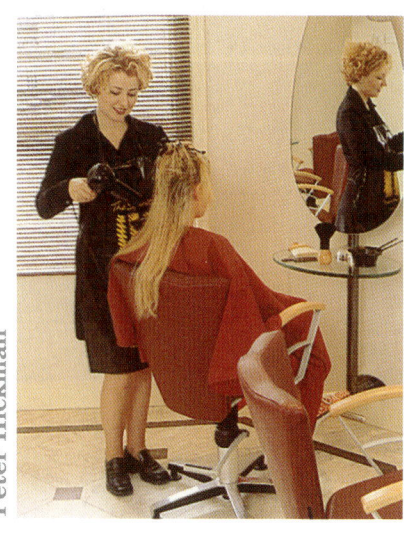

Working together

Remember

There is a huge difference between the friendships that you build out of choice and the others that you have to accept and work with in the professional world.

In element G3.3 Develop Yourself Within the Job Role you should:

- be able to recognise your own strengths and weaknesses at work.
- show that you can find out the correct ways to do tasks when you don't already know.

Key words

Goodwill: the professional bond that is maintained between salon and customer, which is based upon professional communication, trust and respect, ultimately measured by the level of repeated business.

Strengths and weaknesses: a range of abilities which identify the areas; for further development and personal success.

Now try these out!

A salon's success relies on good customer care and teamwork.

Activity

See if you can link the statements on the left with the matches on the right.

Relationships at work are based upon	personal preferences and choice
Friendships outside work are based upon	effective communication takes place
Self development in the job role means	mutual respect and teamwork
Good customer relations occur when	professionalism and personal service
Teamwork takes place when	all the staff do their jobs efficiently
Customer care is built on	making the best of personal strengths and working to improve weaknesses

Activity

How do you communicate with the following staff.

Trainees: ....
....
Stylists: ....
....
The manager: ....
....

Activity

How do you communicate with the following people.

Clients: ....
....
Trade representatives: ....
....
Unknown visitors: ....
....

Creating a good impression with clients

It is vital that you can work well with clients. Right from the point when the clients arrive, you will need to show that you want to help and contribute to their overall satisfaction of the services they receive. You can achieve this by:

- Recognition: remember people and things about them: 'I remember booking your appointment for you last time, following your consultation with Sam'. Always address clients respectfully: you will need to refer to some clients as Mr, Mrs or Miss, whereas younger ones – often students and people you know well – are normally addressed by their first name. Anticipate people's needs, learn to understand the meaning of their posture or body language (see Chapter 3), e.g. when they are happy, sad or angry.

- Listening: really listen and hear what clients say and the way they are saying it. Ask questions if you are unsure or need further clarification.

- Responding: be confident and positive with your actions, give clients your assistance and ask how you could help further. Direct clients to the correct location (waiting area, styling location, backwash or toilets). Offer cups of tea or coffee and find them something to read until the stylist is ready.

Remember

The salon customers are the only reason for the business's existence, without them everything would disappear "as if by magic!"

Lawrain Aumonier at David Aumonier

Always offer clients your assistance; ask how you can help them. If they have an appointment, make sure you take their coat and hang it safely with the others. Tell the stylist the client has arrived and offer a drink and something to read during the wait for the stylist. Simple things like this make all the difference. You are part of the whole service process, providing continuity, benefiting all the team.

Client records

Your salon will probably keep records for clients. These will show:

- personal contact details
- previous treatment history
- products used.

> **Remember**
>
> If a salon keeps client records on computer, the type of information that can be held, and the ways in which it can be used are protected by law, in the Data Protection Act (see page 87 in Chapter 5 for more information on this).

Find the client's details and get them ready for the stylist. When you have found them; check that the contact information is still relevant, up to date and correct.

Sometimes, the information is kept on a computer database. Salons that use computers must take special care of the information they hold. Misuse of clients' personal information is protected by law. The Data Protection Act does not allow anyone to pass on computerised information relating to a client unless the client has expressed permission to do so.

Late arrivals and 'on-spec' appointments

Now and again, a client will arrive late for an appointment. Five minutes here or there is not a problem, the appointment system in any salon has a margin for flexibility.

If a client arrives much later expected, be sympathetic and understanding. Find out if the stylist still has enough time to provide the service. If not, perhaps someone else can attend to the client's needs, but remember to find out how long any additional waiting will be and let the client know.

Conversely, there will always be occasions when a client arrives unexpectedly without an appointment: 'Just on the off chance'. This is good business so be ready to find some way to accommodate these clients. See if anyone is free or available and you can give the client an idea of how long the wait will be.

Now try these out!

> **Activity**
>
> Write down the things that you do when a client arrives at the salon where you work.

What do you do when a client arrives at the salon?
....
....
....
....
....
....
....
....
....
....

Working together 61

Activity

Now think about how you make clients feel appreciated.

What sort of things could you remember about clients that would make them feel appreciated or impressed with your abilities?
....
....
....
....
....
....

Activity

Next, think about your salon's policies.

What is your salon's policy in respect to:

1 Greeting clients when they arrive: ....
....

2 Late arrival for appointments: ....
....

3 Finding and handling client records: ....
....

Supervisor's signature: .... **Date:** ....

WAHL

Activity

How does your salon deal with record keeping?

Q1 What type of client record system does your salon have?
A1 ....

Q2 What information do the records contain?
A2 ....

Q3 When are the records updated?
A3 ....

Supervisor's signature: .... **Date:** ....

Activity

Here is a quick multiple choice quiz, covering a range of salon communications.

Q1 Body language is a form of?
- ❑ verbal communication
- ❑ written communication
- ❑ non-verbal communication
- ❑ verbal and written communication

Q2 Body language is signalled to another person by?
- ❑ posture, gesture and mannerisms
- ❑ smiling
- ❑ maintaining eye contact
- ❑ semaphore

Q3 A client arrives late for her appointment, what do you do?
- ❑ tell her she's too late and ask her if she would like to rebook for another appointment
- ❑ tell her she's late and ask her to take a seat while you tell the stylist
- ❑ seek assistance from a senior staff member
- ❑ ask her to take a seat and seek assistance from a senior staff member

Q4 What client information would not normally be expected to change?
- ❑ title
- ❑ treatment history
- ❑ address
- ❑ telephone/mobile number

Q5 The Data Protection Act protects?
- ❑ the information provider from the data user
- ❑ the data user from the information provider
- ❑ the information provider from the computer
- ❑ the data user from the computer

Q6 What does the Data Protection Act safeguard against?
- ❑ unlawful disclosure of personal information
- ❑ lawful disclosure of personal information
- ❑ safe handling of personal information
- ❑ safe handling of personal computers

Create good working relationships with colleagues

It is important to work well with your fellow salon staff. Breaks or lapses in communication, for whatever reason, can have a critical impact upon the business one way or another. Again, you will need to show that you want to help and contribute to the overall team effort. You can do this by:

- Providing support: teamwork is about collectively making an active contribution. You could seek to help others, even if only passing grips and pins. It is good for staff morale and it shows a good image to the clients.

- Thinking ahead: anticipating the needs of others goes hand in hand with providing support. When you get it right, this anticipation occurs just before support is needed. Perhaps the stylist is doing woven high lights with foils on long hair. You see that there aren't enough foils of a certain length so you go and prepare some more. Just as you finish, the stylist says: 'Could you get me some more foils about 20 cm long please' and you immediately hand them over. Co-operate with the members in your team, make a positive contribution by helping them to provide a well-managed and co-ordinated service. Be self-motivated, keep yourself busy, don't wait to be asked to do things.

- Maintain working harmony: always minimise conflict. Developing working relationships is very different from choosing friends. Although most good working relationships develop quite easily, others need to be worked at. Whatever your personal feelings are about your fellow associates, clients must never sense an atmosphere of tension caused by friction between staff. You get to spend quite a lot of time with the people you work with but you will not always like everyone you meet.

- Respect: people at work have a job to do so, if you are to work as a team, a mutual respect for others is important. Be friendly, helpful and respond to others' requests for help willingly. If you need help, ask in the way that you would wish to be asked.

- Managing your time: making the best use of your time at work is essential. If you manage your time well, things will go smoothly – for you and for everyone else too. Poor use of your time, i.e. not pulling your weight, creates a burden for someone else on the team. As

> **Remember**
>
> Stop, listen and think before doing anything, and if unsure ask! It's easy to charge in and get on with something, when a few more moments could make all the difference between getting it right or getting it wrong.

hairdressing is all about scheduled appointments and running to time so – quite simply – we live by the clock in reception. Get used to the idea right from the start, things can be done either 'just in case' or 'just in time' and these are very different. In 'thinking ahead' we mentioned anticipation – knowing when others are about to need support – in the example above a client is having high-lights. You see that the stylist is about to run out of foils, so you go off to prepare some – just in time.

Still with the same example, if some of the factors of time and accuracy are changed it is easy to see how things could go wrong. Let's say that you see that foils are needed so you go off to prepare some more:

1. You don't find out what lengths are needed so you finish off the rest of the available foil, all at the same short lengths. Now there are no foils of the right length available to finish the job!
2. You try to be helpful and mix up the colours, like last time, on the client's treatment record. It's only after you have mixed them that you realise that the colour choice was changed during consultation. Now product has been wasted, affecting the profitability of the whole job!
3. You see that the high-light foils have been applied so you wash-up the stylist tinting bowls and brushes. A short while later the stylist checks the foils and needs to apply some more. There aren't any of those particular colours left in stock. How can the job be finished?

NI L'Oreal Portfolio

NI L'Oreal Portfolio

Waste is linked to lost profits – a situation that no business wants to be in. As you can see, judging when to do a task is not always easy. The one simple way of ensuring that you don't get the blame, is always to ask if you're not sure.

Now try these out!

Activity

When stylists provide a service to a client they go through set steps – a process – to complete the result. List the steps that you see being performed by the stylists in your salon.

Activity	Stylist	Date
High-lighting		
Retouch colour		
Shampooing		
Conditioning		
Removing tangles from long hair		
Client consultation		
Blow drying		

Supervisor's signature: .... **Date:** ....

Activity

Now think about what actions you would need to ask about and which you would carry out without asking.

What actions would you ask about, before undertaking them, and which would carryout without asking?

Ask about first	No need to ask, just get on with it
....	....
....	....
....	....
....	....

Supervisor's signature: .... **Date:** ....

Activity

What are your salon's disciplinary action and grievance procedures.

Find out you salon's grievance and disciplinary procedures. Summarise them below:

....
....
....

Supervisor's signature: .... **Date:** ....

Activity

Now think about working relationships.

Good working relationships are important because:

....
....
....
....

Building on your own abilities at work

At work, nothing remains the same. If a stylist with a large following of regular clients doesn't continually adapt and improve, the client numbers will fall. Gaining further knowledge and experience might seem hard, particularly after all those years of training, but that's the challenge. Losing more clients than are gained is often difficult to monitor, or bear, but it shows over time. Conversely, winning can be measured by growing popularity, customer loyalty and professional respect.

If you are going to maintain personal success and popularity, you will have to develop on several fronts at the same time:

- Technically: you will have to learn new skills, techniques and applications, and be aware of new developments in hair fashions and product technology.
- Personally: you will need to develop your communication, learning to respond in new situations with new people. You will need to inform others about the new developments, so that clients can benefit from your experience and knowledge. You will also need to communicate well with your team because they will need your support to take them along with the change.

Do you know that: appraisals

Most organisations, small, medium and large, see appraisal as an integrated part of employee development. Appraisal systems will vary from company to company, but all of them use this as a way of: monitoring progress, gathering feedback, setting targets and identifying training needs.

Strengths and weaknesses

Your strengths and weaknesses are the main things that affect the directions of your personal development. Your supervisor will constantly assess your performance – where you are now and where you need to be. The difference between the two is the focus for your personal training and personal action plan. So rather than standing still and remaining the same, you can move forward, change and develop.

Being able to identify your own strengths and weaknesses is fundamental to self-development. If you don't know what you're good at, or what you're not so good at, how can you get any better? Perhaps you have a rough idea in your head of these things. But there are other ways of finding them out and producing a basis for your personal development plan. Self-appraisal and SWOT analysis (this name comes from the words that make up the acronym: strengths, weaknesses, opportunities and threats) are two tried and tested systems for finding out where you are now.

Staff appraisal and reviews

At the beginning of an appraisal session your manager will review your progress to date. This will look at past achievements, personal performance, ability to reach targets and all-round ability to do your job. This information will form the basis of the future appraisal period.

After mutually agreeing the areas of focus, a personal action plan will then be drafted, outlining your new targets.

Sometimes, though, changes might be needed during the appraisal period. In this event, any amendments or modifications to the plan can be jointly discussed, and targets refocused.

The document appraising your performance will contain the following information:

- your name
- the appraisal period
- your appraiser's name and title
- your job title
- your work location
- your agreed performance objectives
- the results you have achieved
- identified areas of strength and weakness – the ongoing action plan
- your overall performance grading.

Self-appraisal

A simple way of evaluating your current abilities is through self-appraisal. You can try this for yourself on page 61. Take some time to complete the details, making sure that you get your work supervisor to check your responses (note: this exercise should be done at regular intervals).

Personal action (or training) plans

We all want to do well at work but how do we know what to do and when to do it? Everyones effectiveness at work can be measured by setting personal targets or goals. Without these targets it would be impossible to know what to work towards, or when you had achieved your goal. So, after completing your self-appraisal and finding your strengths and weaknesses, your supervisor will help you to produce your personal action plan. These mutually agreed action plans:

- provide personalised training targets
- provide timescales for achieving the training targets
- specify any individual training requirements
- confirm future dates for reviewing progress and setting new plans.

The action plan on page 70 is ready for completion.

Self-development

You should take every opportunity to develop yourself at work: you can learn things all the time. Hairdressing takes place in the salon not in a staff room and watching how people do things is one of the best ways to learn. The tasks performed in the salon by stylists and trainees all have one thing in common, they combine two key components – method and knowledge:

- Method is a sequence of steps – done in order – that, when finished, provide a completed process.
- Knowledge comprises the special aspects of the method that need to be understood to reach a satisfactory outcome.

These two things combined are called skills. You can learn skills by watching carefully how things are done and asking questions. Once you have learned the sequences of events that complete the tasks you will be able to demonstrate skills of your own. (These skills, once learned, are seldom forgotten.) You will find that, little by little, you will be broadening the range of your skills and expanding breadth and depth of your knowledge.

Remember

Be organised: make good use of your time. There are always things to be done. Focus on tasks that have to take place before others, e.g. cleaning brushes and equipment, preparing trolleys, tidying reception. If your salon makes certain preparations on a daily basis, make a list of those things so that you always do them when you arrive without having to be asked.

Now try these out!

Activity

Fill in the following self-appraisal form.

Date: ....

Add your comments on how you feel you are progressing in each of the areas listed.

Dealing with clients ....
Reception skills ....
Knowing the products ....
Knowing the services ....
Preparing work areas ....
Cleaning salon equipment ....
Cleaning styling tools ....
Communicating with staff ....
Shampooing ....
Conditioning ....
Neutralising hair ....
Removing high-lights ....
Removing colour ....

Supervisor's signature: ....

Comments: ....
....
....
....

Activity

The following action plan can be used in conjunction with your self-appraisal to provide a focus for personal development. Ask your work supervisor to help you complete it.

Name: .... **Supervisor's name:** ....

Unit	Practical	Date completed	Theory	Date completed

Working together 71

Activity

Now try the following example questions and model assessment answers.

Q1 Why is it important to communicate effectively with salon staff?

A1 Because; you get a clearer understanding of work issues, it builds a rapport and overall it conveys professionalism.

Q2 Why is it important to work within your own job responsibilities?

A2 Because: anything beyond these boundaries, would be unsafe, done wrongly or be incomplete.

Q3 Why is it important to have good working relationships with fellow staff?

A3 Because it helps maintain a friendly, positive and professional working team.

Q4 How do you communicate effectively with your fellow staff members?

A4 By being polite, friendly and helpful. By accurate written communication and positive body language.

Q5 Why is it important to act positively in performance reviews and appraisals?

A5 Because it maintains good working relationships and benefits personal learning and progress.

Activity

Next, match the situations on the left with appropriate courses of action on the right.

Situation	Course of action
A client arrives late	Ask her to take a seat and see if someone has time to attend to her needs
A client arrives without an appointment	Ask her to take a seat in a quieter part of the salon and get a senior to attend to her
Staff absences	See if there is time to still do it or offer a shorter service
A client wants to make a complaint	See if anyone else can handle it first, if not re-book as a last resort

Activity

Finally, rate yourself on the checkerboard.

I understand my job position and how it fits in with the work team ☐	I know why I should always get permission before doing things off my own back ☐	I always follow the salon's policy in respect to client care and customer service ☐	I know who I can turn to if I have any difficulties at work ☐
I know what is expected at work in relation to conduct, attendance and punctuality ☐	I understand the salons grievance procedures ☐	I know the salon's procedures for progress review and performance appraisal ☐	I know how to communicate effectively with staff and customers ☐
I understand the implications of poor client communications ☐	I know how to recognise when clients are happy or angry ☐	I understand principles for identifying my own strengths and weaknesses ☐	I know who can help me with furthering my professional development and training ☐
I know how to make the best use of my time at work ☐			**CHECKER BOARD** ✓

Salon duties and routines

5

Introduction

Providing the service of hairdressing within a salon setting is not just about styling hair. Many things have to be done behind the scenes if clients are to sit in safe, welcoming surroundings and enjoy the whole experience. You will need to show that you can:

- prepare salon materials ready for use
- prepare salon work areas and equipment ready for use.

The unit Prepare for Hairdressing Services and Maintain Work Areas comprises two mandatory elements:

Unit H5
Prepare for hairdressing services and maintain work areas

→ **H5.1** Prepare for salon services

→ **H5.2** Maintain the work areas for haidressing sevices

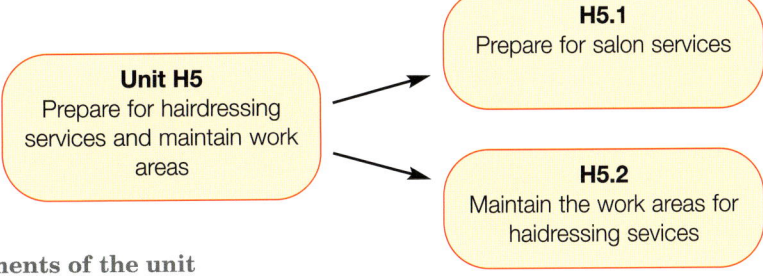

The two mandatory elements of the unit Prepare for Hairdressing Services and Maintain Work Areas

Working in hairdressing involves much more than doing hair. People who come into the salon must be made to feel welcome and confident in the surroundings they see. Businesses try to create an environment and ambience that their clients and potential customers will feel happy to return to again and again; you play a part in that ongoing success.

What do you need to know?

In element H5.1 Prepare for Salon Services you should:

- demonstrate how you prepare salon materials ready for use
- be able to anticipate when things are running out.

L'Oréal Professionnel

In element H5.2 Maintain the Work Area for Hairdressing Services you should:

- show how to clean and tidy the work areas
- be able to check stock levels and replenish when necessary.

Key words

Cross-infection is the way disease is passed on from one person to another.

Sterilisation is a method of eradicating bacteria and disease to prevent any risk of passing on infection.

Salon duties and routines 75

Now try these out!

Activity

Preventing contamination and cross-infection is an important aspect of general health and safety. Link the statements on the left with those on the right.

Antibacterial sprays should be used	for total sterilisation of styling tools by heat
An autoclave is used	for sterilisation by penetrating radiation
Barbicide is a fluid commonly used	on work surfaces and preparation areas
Ultra-violet is	for cleaning sinks and toilets
Household bleach is an effective way	for immersing styling tools into

Activity

Now find out what types and methods of preventing infection are available.

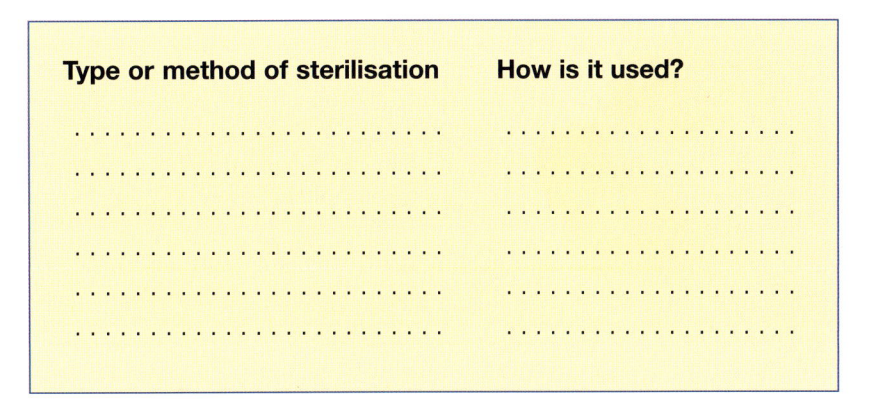

Type or method of sterilisation	How is it used?
....	....
....	....
....	....
....	....
....	....
....	....

Activity

Next, think about what you need to do when you arrive at work.

What things are you expected to do when you arrive at work?

....
....
....
....
....
....

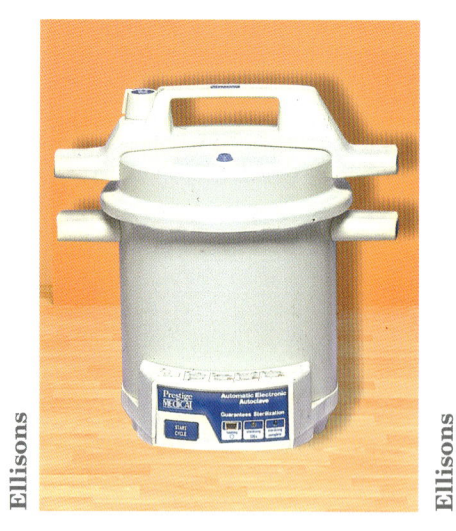

Preventing infection

Earlier in this book (see Chapter 2), we covered those hazards to health and safety that can easily be seen and rectified. However, some hazards cannot be seen, although they create equally important risks to personal health and, like the visible hazards, their impact must be minimised or eliminated.

? Do you know that: infections and disease

We all carry large numbers of micro-organisms inside us, on our skin and in our hair. These organisms – bacteria, fungi and viruses – are too small to be seen with the naked eye. Bacteria and fungi can be seen through a microscope but viruses are too small even for that.

Many micro-organisms are quite harmless but some can cause disease. Those that are harmful to people are called **pathogens**. Flu, for example, is caused by a virus; athlete's foot by a fungus and impetigo by bacteria. Conditions like these, which can be transmitted from one person to another, are said to be **infectious**.

A warm, humid salon can offer a perfect home for disease carrying bacteria. If bacteria can find food in the form of dust and dirt, they can reproduce rapidly. Good ventilation provides a circulating current of air that will help to prevent the growth of bacteria. This is why it is important to keep the salon clean, dry and well aired at all times – and this includes clothing, work areas, tools and all salon equipment.

Sterilisation

Many salons use some form of sterilising system to keep work implements hygienically safe. Sterilisation means the complete eradication of living organisms. The different methods of sterilisation are based on the use of heat, radiation or chemicals.

Autoclaves

These devices provide one of the most effective ways of sterilisation. They work on a principle that is similar to a pressure cooker. Items for sterilisation are heated with a small amount of water inside a pressurised container to a temperature of 125°C for 10 minutes. The high temperature destroys all micro-organisms.

Ultraviolet radiation

Ultraviolet (UV) radiation is an alternative sterilising option. The items for sterilisation are placed in a cabinet fitted with light bulbs that emit UV light, and exposed to the radiation for at least 15 minutes. However, the penetration of UV radiation is low, so sterilisation by this method is not guaranteed.

Chemical sterilisation

Chemical sterilisers should be handled only with suitable personal protective equipment (PPE, e.g. gloves) because many of the solutions used are hazardous to health and should not come into contact with the skin. The most effective form of sterilisation is achieved by the total immersion of the contaminated implements into a bath of fluid (Barbicide is a commonly used brand).

> **Remember**
>
> Infectious diseases should always be treated by a doctor. Non-infectious conditions and defects can often be treated with products available from the chemist.

Now try these out!

Activity

What preparations does your salon make in readiness for opening?

What preparations does your salon make before opening in the morning?

....
....
....
....

Supervisor's signature: .... **Date:** ....

Activity

Now think about where items are kept in your salon.

Where are the following items kept in your salon?

Client gowns: ....

Clean towels ready for use: ....

Towels ready for washing: ....

Cleaning materials: ....

Combs and brushes: ....

Activity

What products are used for general cleaning at work?

The following products are used for general cleaning:

....

....

....

....

Supervisor's signature: .... **Date:** ....

Activity

Now try the following example question and model answer.

Q1 What is the difference between sterilising and disinfecting?

A1 **Sterilising** is a process that eradicates living organisms.

Disinfecting is a routine, day-to-day process for reducing the risk of infection.

Remember

Disinfectants will reduce the probability of infection and are widely used in general day-to-day hygienic salon maintenance.

Antiseptics are used specifically for treating wounds. Many prepackaged first aid dressings are impregnated with antiseptic fluids.

Do you know that: risk assessment

All salons carry out a risk assessment of the substances they use. Any substances that have been identified as potentially hazardous to health will have special handling instructions. These instructions, along with any necessary personal protective equipment (PPE), must be made 'publicly' available within the salon.

General salon hygiene and routine maintenance

Trolleys and trays

The first job of the day, and one that always needs to be done, is preparing the trolleys. Their contents can change several times a day:

- Perm curlers are colour-coded in size order. It is easier for the stylist to ask for a tray to be made up of red/blue and blue/grey curlers than some large ones and some smaller. But before these can be dispensed, they must be thoroughly washed and scrubbed in hot soapy water, this will remove all traces of perming chemicals. After washing they need to be dried thoroughly and any broken or weak rubbers should be replaced.
- Setting rollers/Velcro™ rollers are also colour-coded in size order. These can also be washed, scrubbed and dried in a similar way to perming curlers.
- Salon pins, grips, etc. are easily spilled. It is very wasteful to discard them so make a point of replacing them in their right place.

Remember

Take all possible precautions to avoid dermatitis – use barrier creams and protective gloves whenever possible.

But doing the trolleys in the morning is not enough. Salon trolleys are used as multipurpose workstations throughout the day: the stylists will use them when setting hair, blow drying, tinting and perming. With all this use trolleys tend to need cleaning and tidying several times during the day. However, they are designed with easy cleaning in mind and a simple spray detergent and cleaning cloth will usually do the job.

Floors and seating

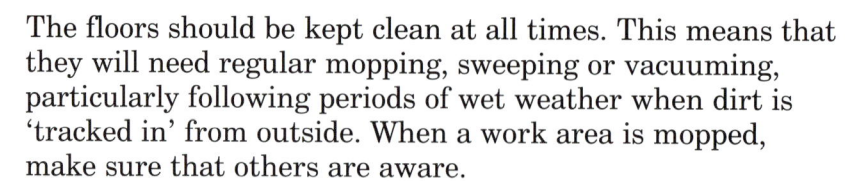

The floors should be kept clean at all times. This means that they will need regular mopping, sweeping or vacuuming, particularly following periods of wet weather when dirt is 'tracked in' from outside. When a work area is mopped, make sure that others are aware.

When using the vacuum cleaner, make a point of checking the collection bag and filters. It doesn't take long for hair clippings to fill the bag, impairing the vacuum's ability to clean properly.

It is much easier to see that vinyl or ceramic floor coverings need cleaning than it is to see that a floor covered in carpet is dirty. If floors need mopping and cleaning, try to do it at a quieter time of the day, probably at the end of the working day so it can dry out totally overnight.

Most salons buy in industrial cleaning products for routine maintenance. These products come in bulk sizes and are far more appropriate for deep, hygienic cleaning than their retail counterparts. Get used to knowing which one does what. More often than not, these products will need to be diluted before use. Always read the manufacturer's instructions before use and remember to wear the correct personal protective equipment. After mopping or waxing floors, dispose of residual fluids in the salon's designated way. Clean the mop thoroughly, rinse well and wring it out before putting it back into store.

Salon styling chairs are made of durable, easy-to-clean materials. Because they are in constant use, the backs of the chairs will often be over-sprayed with hairspray. They should be washed or sponged regularly with hot water and detergent. Don't leave them wet; dry them off with a towel.

The bases of styling chairs need cleaning too. Most chairs have metal or vinyl '5-point star' bases. These should be dusted at least once a day and washed at least once a week. Newer chairs with a hydraulic lift have solid bases, like a barber's chair, and are heavier – normally a metal alloy or chrome. They need cleaning everyday with a suitable spray, followed up by 'buffing' and polishing.

> **Remember**
>
> If you don't know how to change bags and liners, get someone to show you where they are stored and how they are fitted.

> **Remember**
>
> Clear up spillages immediately. If you don't know what it is, ask someone for assistance.

Salon duties and routines

> **Remember**
>
> The salon is a public place and should always present a clean and appealing image to the customer. You have an important part to play in its overall success and remember, a tidy salon is easier to clean, so get into the habit of clearing work areas as and when.

Work surfaces

Preparing the work areas – reception, workstations, backwash and stock preparation areas – means dusting or washing-down at least once each day. Salons tend to have easy-to-wipe surfaces of plastic, glass, tiles or wood. These can be cleaned with spray surface cleaner or hot water and detergent, dried and wiped free of smears.

Now try these out!

Activity

Think about cleaning products.

Which products are used to correctly clean the following?

Wash basins: ....
Glass and mirrors: ....
Carpets and work area floors: ....
Work tops: ....
Brushes and combs: ....

Activity

Now try the following example questions and model assessment answers.

Q1 How often are brushes and combs cleaned?
A1 They are cleaned daily before use

Q2 How are they cleaned?
A2 First of all, any tangles of hair are removed. Then they are washed in hot water and detergent before being dried ready for use.

Q3 Why do stylists discard damaged brushes and combs with missing teeth?
A3 It is unprofessional to use damaged equipment not only because it projects the wrong image to the client but also because it could also tear or damage a client's hair, or at least be uncomfortable.

82 Begin Hairdressing

Activity

Which goes with which?

Remember

Never use scourers or abrasives because these will scratch plastic surfaces. Scratched surfaces deface value and look dull and unattractive, as well as containing minute crevices in which bacteria will develop.

Shampoo		Shines and dusts wood
Spray wax polish		Cleans basins
Metal polish		Cleans hair
Spray bleach		Cleans glasses and cups
Glass spray		Cleans brass
Washing up liquid		Cleans mirrors

Salon duties and routines   83

> **Remember**
>
> Don't try to clean glass with wet cloths or polish – you will spend a long time trying to remove the smears!

Styling mirrors

Glass mirrors should always be sparkling clean! Clients sit in front of the mirrors for the duration of the service and they will not miss those murky smears. The mirrors need to be done every morning before clients arrive and this can be easily done using a window spray cleaner. This will remove all the dirt, dust and hairspray quickly.

Salon equipment

Towels and gowns

Get to know how to use the salon's washing machine and tumble drier. These are in constant use and a quick turn around of laundry will be expected.

Every client must have a fresh, clean towel and gown. These should be machine washed to remove perfume, body odours or staining and to prevent the spread of infection by killing any bacteria.

Styling tools

Combs, brushes and curlers are made from hygienic, easy-to-clean plastics. Combs should be washed daily. If any styling tools are accidentally dropped on to the floor, they cannot be used until they have been re-cleaned. Don't put contaminated items on the work surfaces because they could spread infection.

More and more salons use simple, work-top chemical sterilising jars. These are an efficient way of cleaning implements hygienically between clients: but remember to make sure that the tools are rinsed before use because they have been immersed in to strong chemicals.

> **Remember**
>
> Hairdressers are very sensitive about their scissors: they are a stylist's most important tool. They are expensive and easily damaged if dropped!
>
> **Leave the maintenance to the stylist.**

Hood dryers and colour accelerators

Hood dryers and colour accelerators are made out of tough vinyl mouldings, over metal frames. All these run by electricity and should therefore be handled and cleaned with extreme care. Spray cleaners produce the best results because they expel the minimum cleaning fluid for the optimum cleaning potential. Daily dusting and cleaning at the beginning of the day is fine although, where colour and bleaching products have been used, make sure that the equipment is checked and wiped immediately after use so that staining doesn't occur and clients are not exposed to any hazards.

Hand-held equipment and leads

Hand dryers, tongs, straighteners, hot brushes, etc., can be cleaned when not plugged in and before putting away. Avoid coiling leads as this can weaken the cables and render the equipment either dangerous or useless. Again, all of these items are electrical and should be cleaned with sprays and polish only.

Backwash areas and stock checking

The backwash basins have ceramic finishes, which are hard wearing but brittle. Never put metal, ceramic or glassware items into them because they could crack or be damaged. General cleaning should take place at the beginning of the day, although they will need routine checking every time they are used. This is particularly noticeable around the basin's neck area, especially after clients have had colouring or bleaching services.

Simple spray cleaners containing bleach are an ideal, hygienic solution for both the bowl and chrome mixer valves. Make sure that the hair traps are in place and never pour anything down the drain outlet.

Check the shampoo and conditioner levels at the beginning and end of the day, top these up as and when necessary using a funnel to avoid any wasteful spillages.

Disposing of waste

General salon waste

The everyday items of salon waste (hair clippings, tint tubes and foils, neck wool, food packaging, etc.) should be placed in an enclosed waste bin fitted with a suitably resistant polyethylene bin liner. When the bin is full, the liner can be removed from the bin and sealed using a wire tie. Place in the designated area ready for refuse collection. If for any reason the bin liner punctures, put the damaged liner and waste inside a second bin liner. Wash out the inside of the bin itself with hot water and detergent.

Residual colour and bleach, left over in tint bowls, should be washed out immediately after the stylist has finished the service. These products swell up if left for any period of time and therefore need to be washed away sooner rather than later, as they might increase the risk of blocking the drain.

Disposable razor blades

Used razor blades and similar items should be placed into a safe, screw-topped container. When the container is full it can be discarded. This type of salon waste should be kept away from general salon waste and your local authority might have special disposal arrangements for this 'sharp' waste. Contact the environmental health department at your local council for more information.

> **Remember**
>
> Ask your supervisor at work where you can wash away used colour products. These are hazardous chemicals and your salon might have particular disposal arrangements for this.

Now try these out!

> **Activity**
>
> Salon trolleys: complete the following information.

Q1 How are trolleys prepared at work?
....

Q2 What things are kept in them?
....

Q3 When are they cleaned?
....

Q4 How often should they be cleaned?
....

Activity

Back wash area: complete the following information.

Q1 How are the basins and work areas cleaned?
....
Q2 When should they be cleaned?
....
Q3 When are backwash products checked and refilled?
....
Q4 What is the salon policy for towels and gowns?
....
Q5 What is the salon policy for waste materials and products?
....

Supervisor's signature: .... **Date:** ....

Activity

Now think about the cleaning duties you have performed in you workplace.

What cleaning duties have you performed in your work placement?
....
....
....
....

Supervisor's signature: .... **Date:** ....

Activity

Now try the following example questions and model answers.

Q1 How are setting rollers cleaned and stored ready for use?

A1 Setting rollers can be cleaned by first of all removing the tangled hair by vigorous brushing, then washing in hot soapy water. When they have been rinsed and dried they can be sorted into 'coloured' sizes and put into trolley trays ready for reuse.

Q2 How are perming rods cleaned and stored ready for use?

A2 Perming rods must always be thoroughly washed and dried after each use. Any chemicals left on them from perming and neutralising will affect future use. They are washed in hot soapy water, then dried, the rubbers are checked for deterioration and replaced if necessary. Finally, they are put in size order in trays ready for future reuse.

Finding treatment records

In the past, salons created simple client records for keeping service history and contact details. Traditionally, these were kept in card-index filing systems but, with the growing need to keep more information at hand, many salons now use a computer database. This is far more useful than the old card-index system because computers can find information very quickly. The way in which they search for data enables:

- easy updating and changing of information
- more information to be collected and held on file
- patterns of information to be recognised
- secure, discreet ways of keeping personal data.

The information kept by salons on computer is confidential and must be handled appropriately. The Data Protection Act protects the data source (the client) and penalises the mishandling or breaches of security by the data user (the person accessing the information).

Computer-held information has many benefits over traditional client record systems. The computer is an invaluable tool that can be used for a variety of business needs, e.g. marketing, business development, monitoring client frequency, staff performance and general salon effectiveness.

Keeping client records up to date is essential: out-of-date information is useless and wrong names, contact information or incorrect data negate the whole point of computerising records. So checking the client information has become a routine activity in some salons. Find out what system of client record-keeping your salon uses and see if you can create and find records for other staff.

Activity

Now rate yourself on the checkboard.

I know my salon's work preparation routines ☐	I know my salon's policy in respect to disposing of waste materials and products ☐	I know how to check product levels and refill when necessary ☐	I understand my salon's client recording system and appreciate its importance ☐
I know what things to use for keeping the salon areas hygienically clean and safe ☐	I understand how cross-infection occurs and how to prevent it ☐	I know the methods of sterilisation ☐	I know how to sterilise the various materials used for styling at work ☐
I know the methods of disinfecting ☐	I can handle, use and work with materials, products and equipment safely ☐	I know where materials and equipment is kept at work ☐	
			CHECKER BOARD ✓

Shampooing and conditioning hair

6

Introduction

The services of shampooing and conditioning have a critical impact on the overall satisfaction of the client's visit to the salon. When done properly, these two key services can have an invigorating and stimulating effect or – quite simply – be a wonderful therapeutic experience. You play the vital link in providing this essential component to the total service. You will need to show that you can:

- work safely and carefully on clients to shampoo and condition their hair.

The Shampoo and Condition Hair unit is essential for everyone who works in a salon; it has two mandatory elements:

Unit H1 Shampoo and condition hair

→ **H1.1** Maintain effective and safe methods of working when shampooing and conditioning hair

→ **H1.2** Shampoo and condition hair

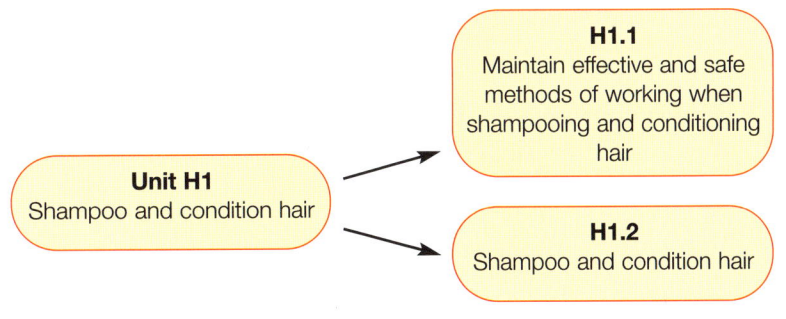

The two mandatory elements of the Shampoo and Condition Hair unit

Shampooing and conditioning are two separate processes that prepare the client's hair for other services. Shampooing is the cleansing process, which removes hairspray, styling products, dirt and grease. The second process – conditioning – improves combing, brushing and flexibility, and adds lustre while improving the hairstyle's overall manageability.

What do you need to know?

In element H1.1 Maintain Effective and Safe Methods of Working When Shampooing and Conditioning Hair you should:

- know how to prepare the client, yourself and the wash area correctly
- discuss how to maintain the wash area.

In element H1.2 Shampoo and Condition Hair you should:

- describe the different massage techniques
- be able to know the difference and applications for your salon's range of shampoo and conditioning products
- demonstrate how to shampoo and condition hair correctly.

Key words

Four different massage techniques are used in shampooing and conditioning:

Effleurage is a gentle stroking movement used in shampooing.

Rotary is a quicker and firmer circulatory movement used in shampooing.

Friction is a vigorous rubbing movement used when shampooing on the scalp areas.

Petrissage is a slower circulatory kneading movement used when applying conditioner.

Now try these out!

Match the shampoos on the right with their appropriate applications (on the left):

Moisturising shampoo	Dandruff
Medicated shampoo	Fine, lank hair
Volumising shampoo	Dry or porous hair
Colour protecting shampoo	Tinted or high-lighted hair

Activity

Shampooing is a process or sequence of events that differs between salons. Write down the preferred shampoo process at your salon. Ask your supervisor to countersign your account.

The sequence of events in the shampooing process in my workplace is:

1 ....
2 ....
3 ....
4 ....

Supervisor's signature: .... **Date:** ....

Activity

Now answer the following questions in the space provided.

Q1 What manufacturer(s) does your salon use for their backwash products?
A1 ....

Q2 What shampoo would you use for dry or porous hair in the salon?
A2 ....

Q3 What shampoo would you use for fine or lank hair in the salon?
A3 ....

Q4 What shampoo would you use for greasy hair in the salon?
A4 ....

Supervisor's signature: .... **Date:** ....

Activity

And finally, answer the following questions in the space provided.

Q1 What conditioner would you use for dry or porous hair in the salon?
A1 ....

Q2 When would it not be appropriate to use conditioner on the hair?
A2 ....

Q3 What benefits does conditioner provide after shampooing?
A3 ....

Supervisor's signature: .... **Date:** ....

Preparations

The purpose of shampooing is to remove dirt, grease or styling products and so leave the hair clean and damp for further processes. Water alone will not break down these particles because they adhere strongly to the surface of the hair. Shampoos contain compounds that can break down this surface tension, allowing the dirt and grease particles to be rinsed away.

Shampoos come in a variety of forms – gels, oils, creams and pastes. Some are milder and gentler on the hair than others. They need different compositions so that they can do their job. Stronger, deeper cleansing shampoos tend to be for greasier hair types. Moisturising shampoos will add much needed moisture and oil to dry, porous hair.

> **Remember**
>
> Regular brushing removes loose hairs and dust or dirt from the hair.

> **Remember**
>
> Frequent-use shampoos are mild enough to be used daily.

Lawrain Aumonier from David Aumonier

Shampooing and conditioning hair

Lawrain Aumonier from David Aumonier

Choosing the right shampoo for the type of hair and following service is very important. If the wrong shampoo is selected the hair might become difficult to handle, fly away, static, brittle or dull. When the hair is to be permed or coloured and the shampoo doesn't remove the styling products from the hair, these could block the action of the chemicals in the technical service and interfere with the overall expected result!

Now try these out!

Activity

Try these example questions and model answers.

Q1 How long should it take to complete the shampoo and conditioning service at work?

A1 We are allowed to take up to 10 minutes for the whole process.

Q2 What is dermatitis and how do you avoid contracting it?

A2 Dermatitis is a skin condition that arises from direct contact with chemical substances. It leaves patchy red areas often between the fingers or over the hands. The areas are itchy and the surface of the skin can break. It can be avoided by wearing barrier creams or thin latex gloves.

Q3 What types of protective wear are available for clients while they are in the salon?

A3 The salon provides gowns, towels and protective capes, which are worn while the services and treatments are provided.

Begin Hairdressing

Activity

Answer the following questions in the spaces provided.

Q1 Why is your posture important when you are shampooing and conditioning?
A1 ....

Q2 What safety considerations do you have to think about while the client is at the basin?
A2 ....

Q3 Why do you have to rinse the hair well after shampooing or conditioning?
A3 ....

Q4 Why do you need to keep the wash area clean and tidy?
A4 ....

Activity

Now think about your salon's policies.

What is your salon's policy in respect to the following procedures:

1 Shampooing and conditioning hair prior to a cut and blow dry?
....

2 Shampooing and conditioning hair prior to a perm?
....

3 Shampooing and conditioning hair after a high-lighting service?
....

Supervisor's signature: .... **Date:** ....

Activity

Use arrows to connect the labelling on the right with the different parts of the hair on the left. Then answer questions A and B.

- The hair root lies at the base of the hair. The skin it is in is attached to the body's blood supply
- The cuticle is the outermost layer of the hair. It is made up of layers that overlap, like the tiles on a roof
- The tip of the hair tapers off to a point on a new hair or hair that has never been cut
- The follicle is a pit in the skin from which the hair grows

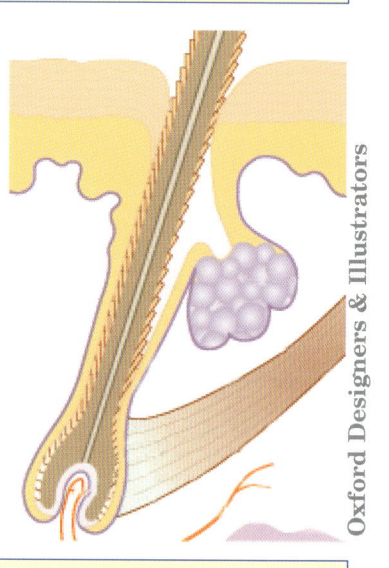

A Which way do the free edges of the cuticle point?
....

B What connection does cuticle have with wet tangled hair?
....

Choosing a shampoo and conditioner

Everyone wants their hair to be in good condition and to be easy to handle. So making the right choice of shampoo and conditioner is essential.

Get it right and the client's hair will be much improved.

Get it wrong and the hair will be difficult to manage or – even worse – longer term damage might occur. The basic choice of product is made on the following factors:

1 Hair type/texture

- Hair washed everyday, needs a mild frequent use shampoo.
- Finer hair needs a gentler or volumising shampoo that doesn't leave it fly away or static.
- Coarse hair needs a shampoo that will make it softer and more pliable.
- Greasy hair should be washed with medicated or an astringent shampoo.
- Dry, porous hair needs added moisture and shine.
- Colour treated hair needs a shampoo to retain the tinted tones.

2 Conditioning benefits to the hair

Good conditioning products protect the hair so that it doesn't lose its natural condition, this allows:

- the hair to be softened and made more flexible
- the hair cuticle to be smoothed
- easier combing and detangling
- damaged parts of the hair to be repaired
- better reflection of light, denoted by shine and lustre
- the hair to be chemically rebalanced to its natural, mildly acid state.

Remember

Always ask the stylist which type of shampoo and conditioner are required. The wrong product used could jeopardise the subsequent service.

3 The service or treatment to follow

What the stylist will be doing next has a great bearing on which products should be used. Some shampoos and most conditioners contain 'waxy' or oily compounds that coat the hair. This can be very useful for improving the hair for blow drying but would disadvantage a chemical treatment like a perm or some colour services. The stylist will always tell you which shampoo is needed and whether conditioner is required.

> **Do you know that: dandruff**
>
> Dandruff is a common scalp disorder. Normally, the skin cells produced in the lower dermis take 35–45 days to work up through to the surface of the epidermis. Once there the cells are shed daily in the form of a fine visible dust.
>
> In the case of dandruff, this process becomes erratic. The cells of the epidermis are shed in clumps in the form of visible white flakes. These changes are the result of the shedding process taking place too rapidly due to the increased production of epidermal cells.
>
> There are two types of dandruff: dry dandruff (pityriasis simplex), which appears as fine, dry, brownish flakes, and greasy dandruff (steatoid pityriasis), which is associated with a greasy scalp and has thick yellowish, greasy scales that stick to the scalp.
>
> Dandruff is caused by an excess build-up of microbial yeast upon the scalp. This yeast, present on all scalps, will cause itching and inflammation. This in turn will increase cell production and hence more epidermal cells are renewed and more dandruff sheds away.
>
> Successful antidandruff shampoos and conditioners contain chemicals that control the yeast production, ease the itching and inflammation and slow down the cell renewal process.

Shampooing the client

Successful shampooing is easy as long as you remember the process:

1. Sit the client at the basin and help him or her into a clean, fresh gown.
2. Place a freshly laundered towel around the neck and across the shoulders.
3. Adjust the basin so that when the client's head is tilted back the position is comfortable with the minimum of towel supporting the neck.
4. Carefully disentangle the hair: initially by working the fingers through the lengths and then by brushing with a wide-toothed brush.
5. Turn on the water and control the mixture of hot and cold. Test the temperature on the back of the hand to make sure the temperature is neither too cold or hot.
6. Place one hand across the brow of the hairline, 'damming' the water from splashing forward onto the face. Start rinsing the hair from the forehead, down

Shampooing and conditioning hair | 97

> **Remember**
>
> Make sure that the client is comfortable throughout the shampoo/conditioning process.

either side, cupping the ears and through to the lengths.

7 Check the flow of water pressure and temperature regularly throughout.
8 After the hair is thoroughly wet, apply a small amount of the correct shampoo to the palms of the hand, lightly rub together and then apply evenly to the client's hair.
9 With the fingers clawed, massage the scalp with the correct massage technique. Cover the whole scalp and maks sure that you don't miss any.
10 Rinse the hair thoroughly, checking water temperature and pressure.
11 If the stylist requires two washes, repeat steps 5–10.
12 Rinse all traces of shampoo lather away form the hair and lightly squeeze out the excess water. If the stylist does not require any conditioner the client can now be gently seated upright and the edges of the towel placed across the hairline and secured in place.

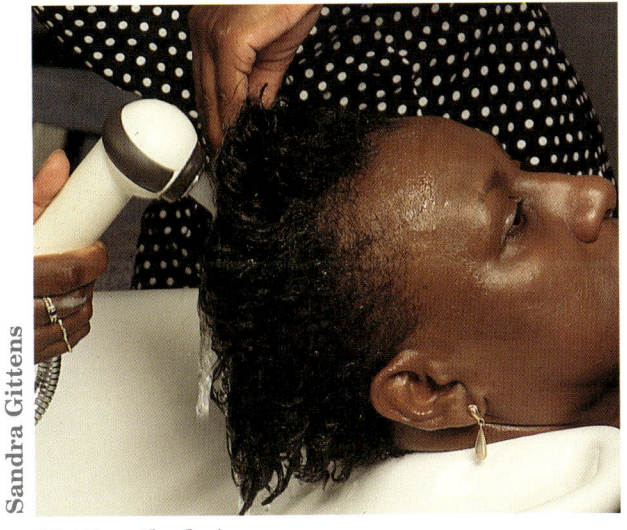

Wetting the hair

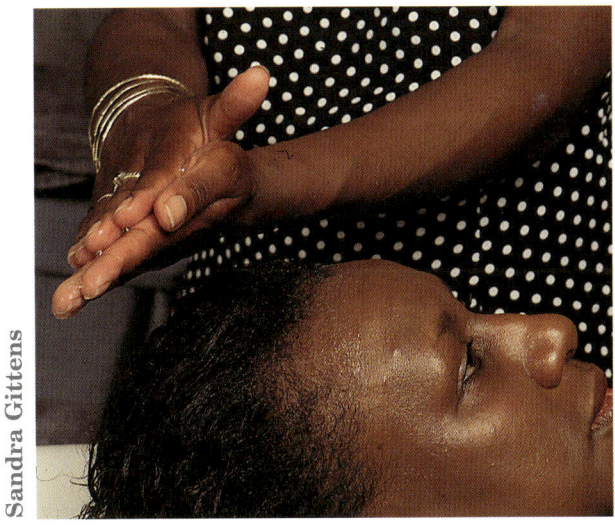

Spreading shampoo over the palms

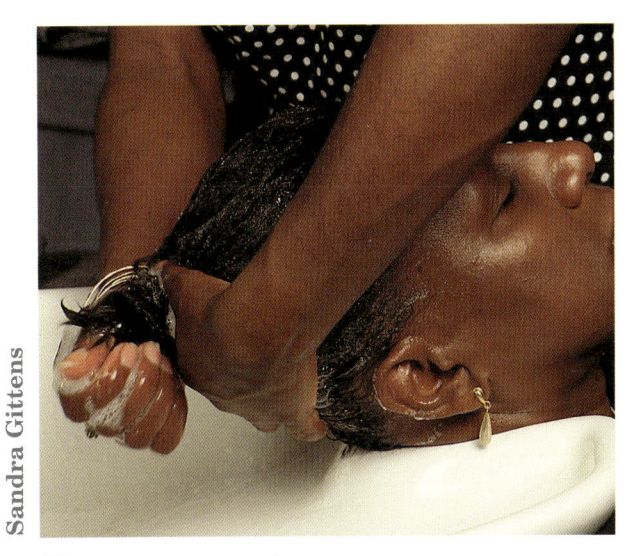

Distributing the shampoo throughout the hair using effleurage movements

Begin Hairdressing

Pushing the fingers under the hair and massaging the scalp

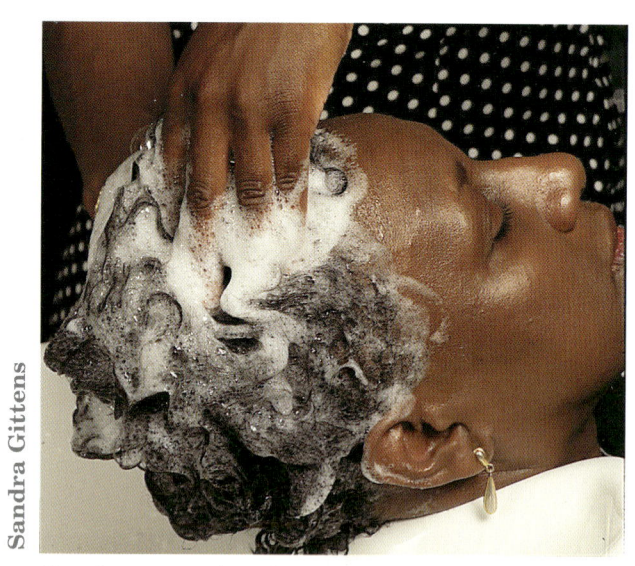

Gently massaging the scalp

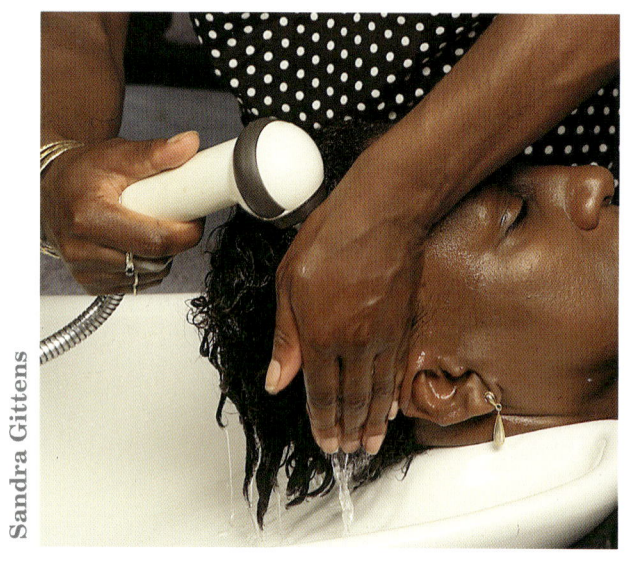

Rinsing the hair

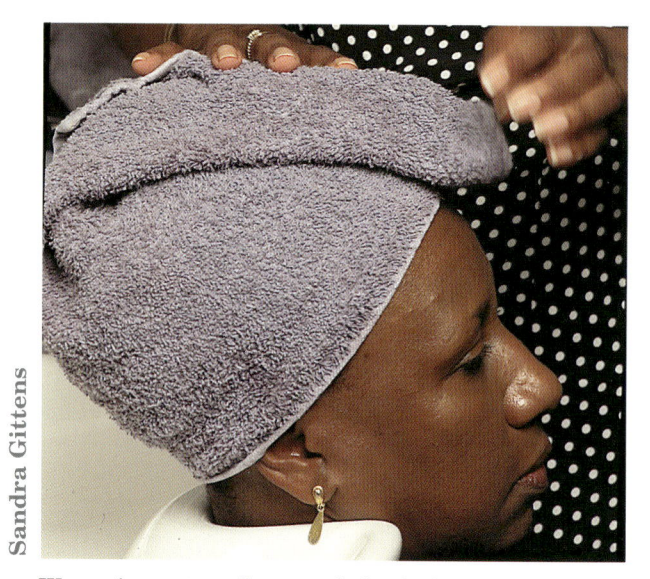

Wrapping a towel around the hair

The different types of massage techniques

There are three type of shampooing technique and one other suitable for conditioning treatments:

- Begin shampooing with effleurage movements – gentle stroking movements (see figure).
- Continue with rotary movements – let the finger-tips glide over the scalp while moving your hands towards each other in the centre (up from the sides, over the top and down into the nape of the neck). Use smaller, quicker circular movements than for effleurage.
- Occasionally change to friction techniques to deep clean any difficult areas. Use quick rubbing movements.
- After shampooing, petrissage is used during conditioning to apply the product to the hair and scalp. Use slow, deep kneading movements.

Effleurage movement

Conditioning the client

Conditioning follows on from the shampoo process in most salon situations. When shampooing is finished, and with the client remaining at the basin, a surface conditioner can be applied. Unlike penetrating conditioners, these types of conditioner remain on the outer, cuticle layer of the hair improving combing, manageability and enhancing the appearance of the hair:

1. Squeeze out excess moisture from the hair.
2. Put a small amount of conditioner in the palm of your hand and gently rub your hands together, applying the conditioner – evenly – to as wide a surface area of your hand as possible.
3. On longer hair – apply the conditioner to mid-lengths and ends first, working through the hair with the fingers, separating the lengths.
4. On shorter hair – evenly apply the conditioner to all of the hair.
5. Start the petrissage movements over the scalp – work from the frontal area, over the top and down through to the nape of the neck. Repeat this circulatory process several times.
6. On longer hair that is in poorer condition, you might need to comb the conditioner through while still at the

Remember

When disentangling long hair, always work from the points of the hair first, working backwards up the hair, towards the roots. This:

1 makes combing far easier and quicker
2 eliminates harsh, painful pulling
3 reduces tearing and further damage to the hair
4 minimises any discomfort to the client.

basin. Using a wide tooth conditioning comb start disentangling the hair working at the points of the hair first, then gradually working a little further up the hair, until the hair can be combed easily from roots to ends.

7 Rinse all traces of conditioner away from the hair and lightly squeeze out the excess water.
8 Place the towel around the hair, secure into place and move the client to the styling section.
9 Place another fresh towel around the shoulders and remove the damp one squeezing out the excess moisture from the lengths.
10 Disentangle the hair with a wide-toothed comb until all tangles are free from the hair.

Now try these out!

Activity

Look at the following example questions and model answers.

Q1 Why is it important to keep checking the water temperature during shampooing and conditioning?
A1 The temperature of the water could change and easily cause the client discomfort.

Q2 Why should you turn the water off between washes?
A2 It minimises wastage; water costs money.

Q3 Why is it important to regulate the flow of water?
A3 If the water pressure is to high it will splash the client.

Activity

What would happen in the following situations?

What happens if:

Q1 You shampooed the client's hair with the wrong product?
A1 ....

Q2 You conditioned the client's hair with the wrong product?
A2 ....

Q3 You didn't rinse the hair thoroughly enough after conditioning?
A3 ....

Activity

Self-assessment for shampooing and conditioning.

I know what the effleurage movement is and when to use this massage technique?
Yes ☐   No ☐

I know what the rotary movement is and when to use this massage technique?
Yes ☐   No ☐

I know what the friction movement is and when to use this massage technique?
Yes ☐   No ☐

I know what the petrissage movement is and when to use this massage technique?
Yes ☐   No ☐

I know why and how to de-tangle client's hair properly?
Yes ☐   No ☐

I know how to dispense the right amount of shampoo product for a client?
Yes ☐   No ☐

I know how to dispense the right amount of conditioning product for a client?
Yes ☐   No ☐

I can regulate the water pressure and temperature properly?
Yes ☐   No ☐

Supervisor's signature: . . . .   **Date:** . . . .

Activity

True or false.

Hair should always be shampooed twice
True ☐   False ☐

The free edges of the cuticle always point towards the tip of the hair
True ☐   False ☐

One shampoo tends to be very similar to another
True ☐   False ☐

All conditioners work on the surface of the hair
True ☐   False ☐

Dermatitis can be caused by shampooing hair
True ☐   False ☐

Dandruff is a scalp condition
True ☐   False ☐

Activity

Now rate yourself on the checkboard.

I know how to prepare clients correctly ☐	I know how to check stocking levels and who to tell in the event of shortages ☐	I can always shampoo and condition any client's hair within 10 minutes ☐	I know the massage techniques and when they are used ☐
I know how dermatitis can occur and how it is avoided ☐	I understand the implications of backwash product in relation to personal health and safety ☐	I always make sure that the client is comfortable throughout shampooing and conditioning hair ☐	I know how to communicate effectively with staff and customers ☐
I understand the implications of poor cleaning and hygiene ☐	I know how to shampoo and condition a wide range of hair lengths and types correctly ☐	I always follow the stylist's instructions ☐	I know what surface conditioning is and the benefits to the client's hair ☐
I know why the wastage of salon resources should be minimised ☐			**CHECKER BOARD** ✓

Helping with perms, relaxing and colour processes

Introduction

This chapter covers the duties surrounding the chemical-technical operations of neutralising perms, relaxing hair and the removal of colours and high-lights. These processes are vital for a successful conclusion of the service and ultimately the satisfaction of the client. The NVQ unit requires you to do one of the three options below. You will need to show that you can:

- help with perming and colouring services
- or help with perming, relaxing and colouring services
- or help with perming, relaxing and colouring services for African–Caribbean hair.

Option 1: the unit Assist with Perming and Colouring Services comprises three elements:

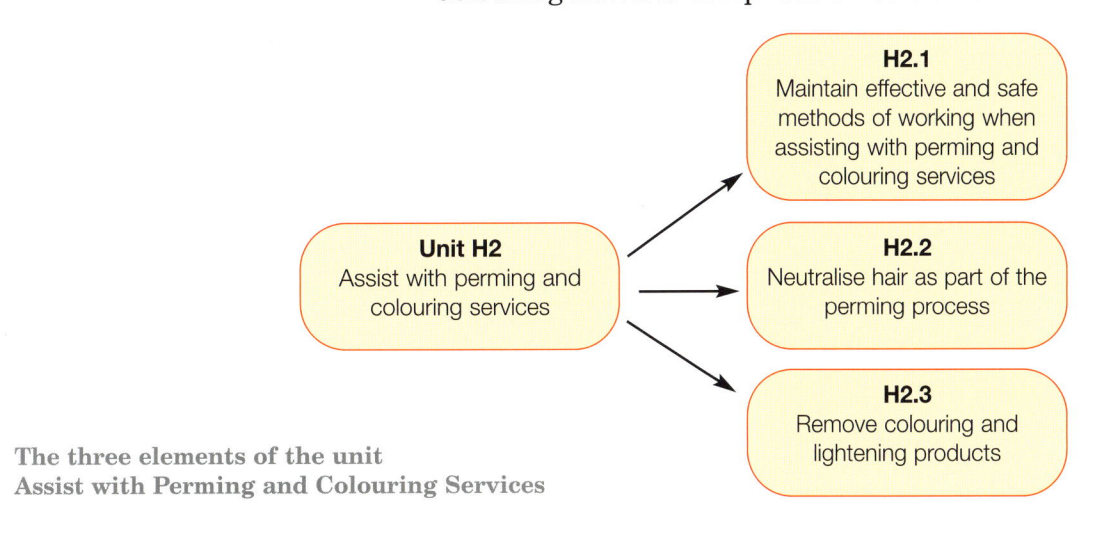

Unit H2 Assist with perming and colouring services

- **H2.1** Maintain effective and safe methods of working when assisting with perming and colouring services
- **H2.2** Neutralise hair as part of the perming process
- **H2.3** Remove colouring and lightening products

The three elements of the unit
Assist with Perming and Colouring Services

Option 2: the unit Assist with Perming, Relaxing and Colouring Services comprises three elements:

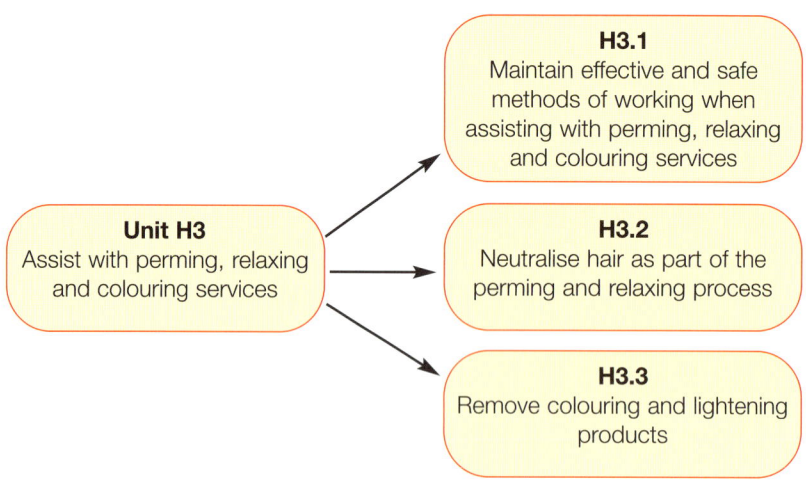

Unit H3 — Assist with perming, relaxing and colouring services

- **H3.1** Maintain effective and safe methods of working when assisting with perming, relaxing and colouring services
- **H3.2** Neutralise hair as part of the perming and relaxing process
- **H3.3** Remove colouring and lightening products

The three elements of the unit Assist with Perming, Relaxing and Colouring Services

Option 3: the unit Assist with Perming, Relaxing and Colouring Services for African–Caribbean hair comprises three elements:

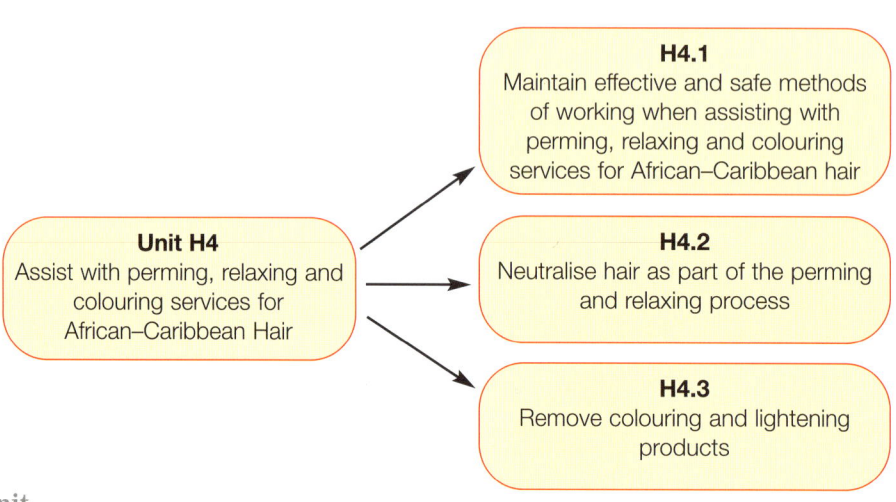

Unit H4 — Assist with perming, relaxing and colouring services for African–Caribbean Hair

- **H4.1** Maintain effective and safe methods of working when assisting with perming, relaxing and colouring services for African–Caribbean hair
- **H4.2** Neutralise hair as part of the perming and relaxing process
- **H4.3** Remove colouring and lightening products

The three elements of the unit Assist with Perming, Relaxing and Colouring Services for African–Caribbean Hair

These services complete a range of chemical technical processes. They are as vital as the work undertaken by the stylists. This chapter contains the information for all three units: **remember, you need to choose only one option to complete the hairdressing NVQ level 1.**

Helping with perms, relaxing and colour processes | 105

What do you need to know?

In unit H2 element H2.1, unit H3 element H3.1 and unit H4 element H4.1, Maintain Effective and Safe Methods of Working when assisting with:

1 perming and colouring services
2 perming, relaxing and colouring services
3 perming, relaxing and colouring services for African–Caribbean hair.

- You need to know how to prepare the client, yourself and the work area correctly.
- You need to know how to work safely when dealing with chemical processes.

George Paterson SA Hairdressing

George Paterson SA Hairdressing

In unit H2 Element H2.2 Neutralise Hair as Part of the Perming Process you need:

- to be able to carry out the neutralising process according to manufacturer's instructions
- to understand the chemical changes taking place during the process.

Additionally; in unit H3 element H3.2 and unit H4 element H4.2 you will need to be able to:

- neutralise the hair after a relaxing process.

And finally, In Unit H2 element H2.3, unit H3 element H3.3 and unit H4 element H4.3 Remove Colouring and Lightening Products you need to know that:

- different colour products work in different ways
- the removal of different colouring services need to handled in different ways.

Helping with perms, relaxing and colour processes   107

Aa Key words

Here are a number of terms used within hairdressing:

Neutraliser (or normaliser) is a chemical compound which is used to both balance and fix hair that has been previously permed or relaxed.

Semi-permanent colour is a type of hair dye that lasts until it fades off the hair.

Permanent tint is a type of hair dye that penetrates deeper into the hair than semi-permanents lasting until it grows out.

Powder bleach is a product that is used to remove natural hair colour, commonly used in high-lighting.

Colour retouch a service, whereby the client has only the roots tinted to match previous colour on the ends.

High-lights/low-lights a service whereby the client may have one or more tints and/or bleach applied to the hair, to create a multi toned effect.

Relaxing is a process whereby natural wave is reduced producing a straighter effect.

Now try these out!

Activity

Match the chemical services on the left with their appropriate meanings on the left.

- **Permanent wave** — A technical service involving the permanent rearrangement of bonds within the hair in order to eliminate wave

- **Relaxing** — A technical service whereby parts of the hair are toned to produce a varied coloured effect

- **High-lighting** — A technical service involving the permanent rearrangement of bonds within the hair in order to produce wave

- **Retouch colour** — A roots-only application of permanent colour

Activity

True or false.

Neutraliser is used in a perm service to fix wave into hair
True ☐   False ☐

Neutraliser is used in a relaxing service to fix wave into hair
True ☐   False ☐

Hydrogen peroxide is a permanent tint
True ☐   False ☐

The colour of hair is derived from very small pigments
True ☐   False ☐

The natural colour of hair is derived from very small pigments
True ☐   False ☐

Neutraliser contains hydrogen peroxide
True ☐   False ☐

Hair dyes are the same as fabric dyes
True ☐   False ☐

Activity

Match the chemical products on the left with the effects they have on hair (right).

Bleach	A product that deposits synthetic pigments onto the surface of the hair
Semi-permanents	A product that deposits synthetic pigments deep into the hair shaft
Permanent tint	A product for removing natural pigments from the hair
Hydrogen peroxide	A product used in conjunction with permanent tint or bleach, as part of the development process

Activity

Now try the following example questions and model answers.

Q1 Why is neutraliser an essential part to the perming process?
A1 Without it the wave or curl formed by the perm would drop out

Q2 Why is timing critical to the neutralising process?
A2 If the neutraliser is not left on long enough the perm will fade and drop out. If it is left on too long, the condition of the hair will deteriorate proportionally to length of over-processing

Helping with perms, relaxing and colour processes | 109

Process overviews

Perming/neutralising

Information about preparing the work area, the materials and the client appears elsewhere within the text. To avoid any unnecessary repetition, only new information is given in this chapter.

The process of perming, which is always carried out by a stylist, is a highly technical aspect of hairdressing. The service involves the placing and positioning of rods/curlers into the client's hair, to which a perming solution is applied. After a period of development a test curl is taken to determine the processing of the hair. If the development is complete, the permed hair is fixed and chemically rebalanced by the process of neutralising.

Neutralising always takes place at the basin, any plastic caps, capes or cotton wool are carefully removed and damp towels are replaced. The client is made comfortable and the hair is rinsed thoroughly. Rinsing with warm water removes the perming chemicals from the hair, taking special care not to dislodge any of the curlers or rods, etc.

After rinsing, the saturated hair is blotted with a dry towel until it is just slightly damp. The neutraliser is applied (following the manufacturer's instructions) and left on for the appropriate timing. The rods are then carefully removed and more neutraliser is applied to the mid-lengths and ends. After this, the hair is rinsed thoroughly to remove any excess chemicals and conditioner and, before the client sits back at the styling unit, the hair is carefully lifted to remove any tangles before the stylist resumes the styling process.

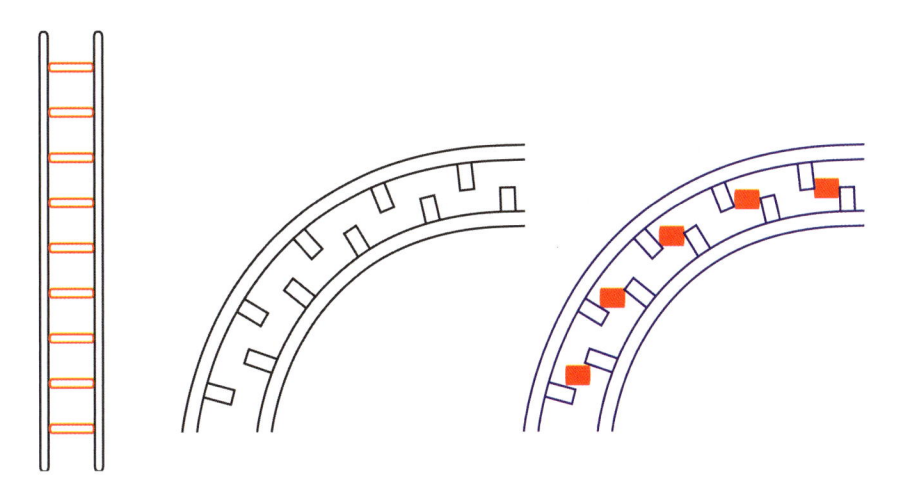

Remember

Your salon will have its own ways of neutralising, find out what they are and how you are expected to do it.

The ladder analogy

> **? Do you know that: how perms work**
>
> The chemical actions and reactions that take place within the hair during processing involve some complex chemistry. A simple analogy to explain the changes that take place within the hair during perming and neutralising is to use a simple wooden ladder as an example.
>
> If you imagine a ladder represents a single hair, the strength of the ladder is in the two long uprights. However, when climbing up the ladder, it flexes. So although strong and rigid, it is capable of movement. The strength and shape of the ladder is derived from the rungs. Each rung is evenly spaced holding the main structure of long uprights apart. These rungs are like the disulphide bonds in the hair shaft. These linkages give natural hair its strength.
>
> During perming, a solution of ammonium thioglycolate is added to the hair after the curlers have been wound in. The solution breaks the disulphide bonds chemically, just as if you had taken a saw and cut through all the rungs. So if you imagine that the ladder is now bent, the rungs now don't line up, the cut rungs have changed positions.
>
> The next part of the perming process – neutralising – re-fixes the bonds by adding a solution enriched with oxygen. Just like the bent ladder, the rungs are glued together in the new, reformed shape and – just like perming – if the gluing is done well the ladder remains in a permanent, bent shape. If it is done poorly the ladder springs back to a straighter shape.

Relaxing hair

Relaxing wavy hair works in much the same way as perming, but in reverse! During this procedure naturally wavy hair is made straighter. The hair is stretched either by winding it on very large curlers or by combing. When the hair is straight, a relaxing solution is added to break the disulphide bonds (see above). After development, the hair is neutralised and the bonds are permanently reformed in the new positions to give a straighter result.

Removing colours and lighteners

Hair colourants are not like paint and they should not be used like it either! Rather than just colouring the surface of the hair, today's popular colours and more preferred effects work deep inside the hair shaft. This complex chemistry can:

Helping with perms, relaxing and colour processes

Remember

When shampooing in preparation for perming, always check with the stylist which shampoo you should use. Some shampoos are unsuitable for perming because they can leave a protective build-up on the hair. This can affect the ability of the perming chemicals to work within the hair.

- add new tones, e.g. red, gold, mahogany, to natural hair
- make natural hair darker
- make previously coloured hair darker
- remove natural pigments making hair lighter
- combinations of all of these at the same time.

So, different colouring products work in different ways. Taking colours off is not as straightforward as you might think. Different colour processes need to be handled in different ways, and this is especially true when two or more colours are to be removed. Lack of care and attention here will result in a very undesirable conclusion. It is vital that you know what you have to do and that you understand what is being done before attempting any colour removal.

Now try these out!

Activity

Neutralising a perm: put the following in the right order by numbering the boxes.

- ☐ The hair is rinsed thoroughly to remove the perm chemicals.
- ☐ The water temperature is checked and pressure controlled.
- ☐ The curlers are removed and more neutraliser is applied to the ends carefully so not to disturb the newly permed hair.
- ☐ The client is seated at the basin and any caps, shoulder capes, cotton wool or damp towels are removed and replaced as necessary.
- ☐ The correct neutralising product is applied to the wound curlers and left for the appropriate time.
- ☐ The saturated hair is blotted with a towel until slightly damp.
- ☐ A final rinsing removes all excess product from the hair and a clean fresh towel is applied.

Activity

Removing a root colour: put the following in the right order by numbering the boxes.

- ☐ Conditioner is applied and worked through to the ends.
- ☐ The water temperature is checked and water pressure controlled.
- ☐ A final rinsing removes all excess product from the hair and a clean fresh towel is applied.
- ☐ Warm water is applied evenly over tinted the hair and then massaged into an emulsion to help release tint from the hair.
- ☐ The hair is rinsed and shampooed again if necessary.
- ☐ The hair is gently shampooed using the correct massage techniques.
- ☐ The correct shampoo is selected and a little is evenly applied to the palms of the hands.
- ☐ The client is seated at the basin and any caps and shoulder capes are removed.

Activity

Removing high-lights: put the following in the right order by numbering the boxes.

- ❏ The appropriate secondary colour high-light foils are unwrapped and rinsed individually and thoroughly to remove all traces of product from the hair.
- ❏ The client is seated at the basin and any caps and shoulder capes are removed.
- ❏ The water temperature is checked and water pressure controlled.
- ❏ When all the high-lights are removed from the hair, the correct shampoo is selected and a little is evenly applied to the palms of the hands.
- ❏ The appropriate first colour high-light foils are unwrapped and rinsed individually and thoroughly to remove all traces of product from the hair.
- ❏ Before moving the client to the basin, check with the stylist the order in which the high-light should be removed (lightened or tinted hair, which ones first, second and so on?).
- ❏ The hair is rinsed and shampooed again if necessary.
- ❏ The hair is gently shampooed using the correct massage techniques.
- ❏ A final rinsing removes all excess product from the hair and a clean fresh towel is applied.
- ❏ Conditioner is applied to the hair and worked through to the ends.

George Paterson SA Hairdressing

Helping with perms, relaxing and colour processes 113

Desmond Murray

Anthony Holland @ Zullo & Pack, Nottingham

Activity

Multiple choice quiz.

Q1 The bonds that are broken within the hair during the action of perming are:
- ammonium thioglycolate
- disulphide bonds
- oxygen
- none of the above

Q2 The neutralising agent will:
- recondition the hair
- reform the bonds within the hair
- replace the perm solution
- have no effect on permed hair

Q3 Neutraliser is a chemical product containing
- ammonia
- bleach
- oxygen
- sulphur

Q4 Relaxing and perming are similar because:
- bonds within the hair are broken and refixed into new permanent positions
- straight and curly hair is the same
- bonds within the hair are unaffected
- straightening and curling is the same

Q5 The action of tinting hair will:
- add tone to natural colour
- add bleach to natural colour
- remove synthetic hair colour
- remove bleach from natural colour

Q6 The action of lightening hair will:
- add tone to natural colour
- add depth to natural colour
- remove natural hair colour
- remove bleach from coloured hair

Working with different products

A great number of products have been developed for perming, relaxing and neutralising. Hair types around the world vary greatly and products have been developed accordingly to accomodate these differences. Celebrities from the world of music and entertainment often popularise hairstyles that the general public then wish to emulate. In order for the same style to be achieved, each hair type relies upon the application of a variety of products and a range of techniques specifically suited to it.

Although the outcomes are the same, each technical procedure requires great care, attention and safe handling. The products involved are strongly alkaline or acidic, they are a potential hazard to you and the client, so extra care must be taken when they are used.

The ways in which the technical processes are carried out for perming, relaxing and neutralising different hair types varies very little: either curlers are put in or product is applied directly to the hair and combed through. Techniques do differ, though, after neutralising relaxer treatments on African–Caribbean hair types.

So when stylists put curl into straight hair, they wind curlers into their client's hair and apply lotion directly onto these to perm the hair. A lotion is used because it has a better chance of absorption by the hair wound around the curler.

Using curlers and lotion to put curl into straight hair

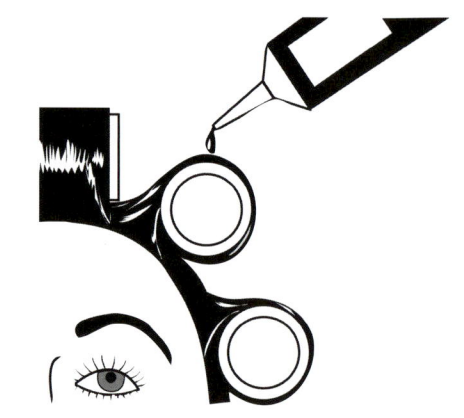

> **Remember**
>
> Manufacturers often match their products together.
>
> Always check that you are using the right chemical for the service. Perm solutions, relaxers and neutralisers contain ingredients that need to be chemically balanced or counteracted.

Conversely, when curl is being removed from hair in a relaxer treatment, say in straightening African–Caribbean hair, a cream-based product is used because it sticks to the hair better. This makes for easier handling, improved safety and guarantees better results. When the treatment has developed, the relaxer is neutralised with a neutralising shampoo that re-forms the bonds in the hair in a straighter state and helps to remove the cream relaxer.

Helping with perms, relaxing and colour processes   115

Neutralising

After a perm

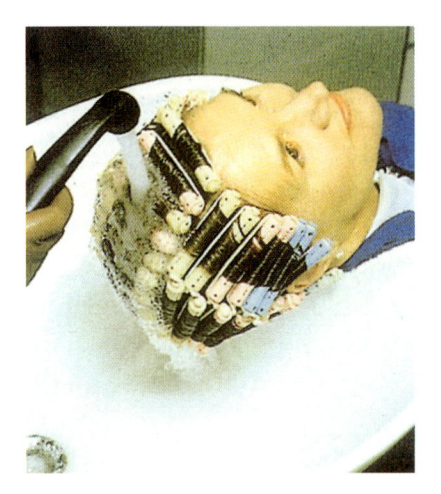

1 When the perming process is complete, move the client to the basin and carefully remove any cotton wool, plastic caps and shoulder capes. Change the towel for a clean, fresh one.

2 Regulate the flow of water and the temperature so that the water pressure is moderate. The water must not be too hot because the client's scalp might have been sensitised by the perm process. Put on your latex gloves.

3 Rinse the hair thoroughly for at least 5 minutes. This stops any further development of the perm and removes all traces of perm solution from the hair. Take care not to splash water on the client or dislodge any curlers. (If any come loose tell the stylist immediately so they can be re-tightened or replaced.)

4 After rinsing, blot all the curlers thoroughly with a towel, making sure to get down to the lower ones at the neck.

5 After all excess moisture is removed, apply the neutraliser in line with manufacturer's instructions. Sometimes you will apply it by sponge, sometimes by brush and sometimes straight from the applicator. Mop up any spillages around the hairline as you go with damp cotton wool.

6 When all the hair has been covered, leave the hair to process for the correct time (usually 5–10 minutes).

7 Carefully remove the curlers without stretching the curls, apply the second application of neutraliser and leave for a further few minutes.

8 Rinse thoroughly until all traces are gone then condition appropriately.

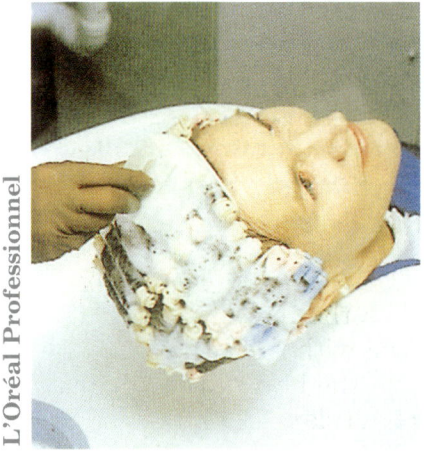

Rinse hair thoroughly

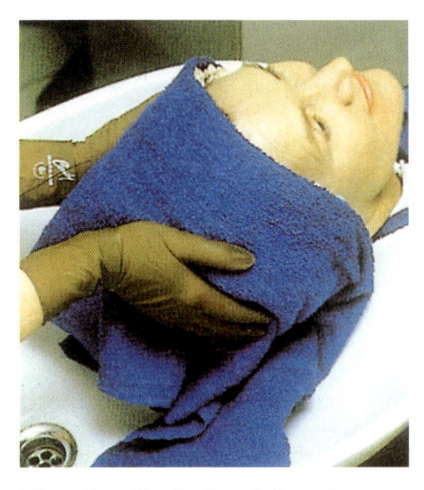

Blot dry the hair with a clean, fresh towel

Apply the neutraliser

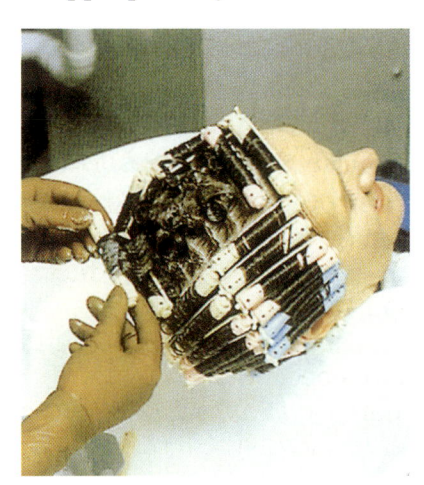

Carefully remove the curlers without stretching

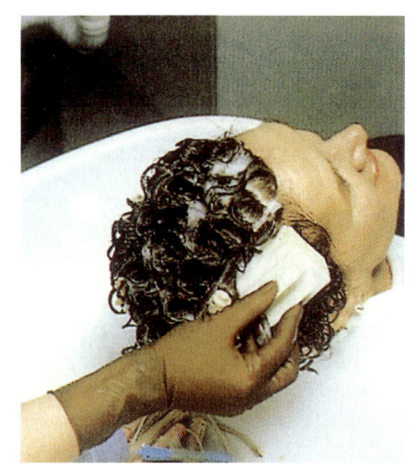

Re-apply a second application of neutraliser

L'Oréal Professionnel

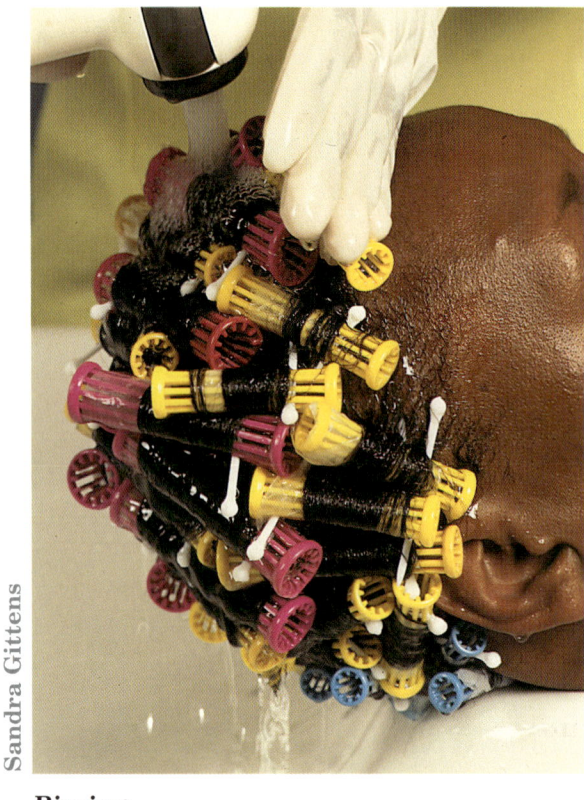

Rinsing

After a relaxer

1. When the relaxing process is complete, move the client to the basin and remove the shoulder cape and replace with a fresh towel.
2. Put on your gloves and rinse the hair thoroughly with tepid water to remove the cream relaxer.
3. While you are rinsing, carefully massage the hair and scalp to help remove all the chemicals without rubbing.
4. When all the product has been removed, apply the neutralising shampoo to the hair. Make sure that all areas have been massaged and then rinse thoroughly.
5. Reapply and repeat the shampoo process again; finally rinse well.
6. Towel-dry the hair and carefully remove any tangles.

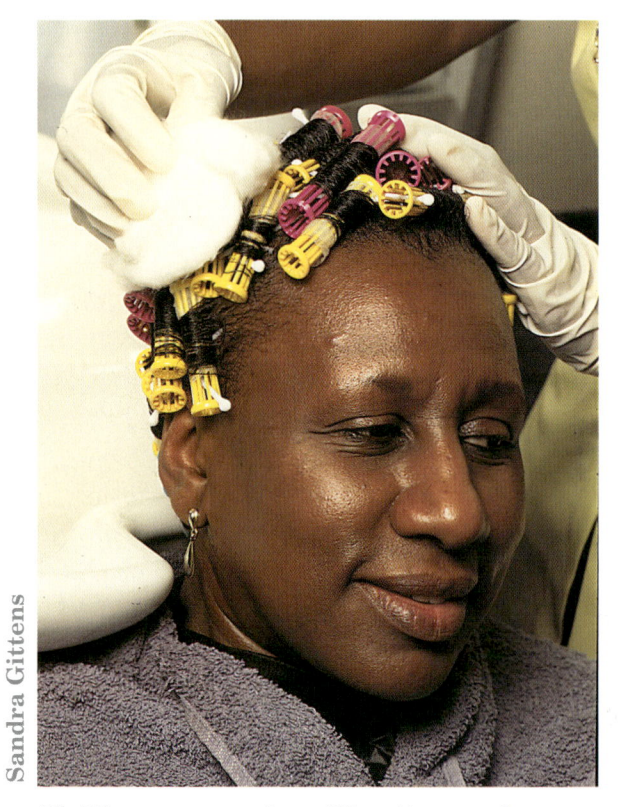

Towel-drying

Blotting excess water with cotton wool

Helping with perms, relaxing and colour processes

Applying neutraliser

After removing rods

Colour removal

Removing (a single) colour from hair

Colouring products for hair tend to fall into four general groups:

1 Temporary colour: often applied as mousse or setting lotion, lasts until the hair is washed next.
2 Semi-permanent colour: often applied from an applicator or shampooed into the hair, it lasts up to 6–8 washes with some fading but without re-growth.
3 Permanent colour: always mixed with a developer, it is usually applied with a brush or straight from an applicator to the hair, it lasts until it grows out.
4 Lighteners: sometimes in the form of a bleach, mixed with a developer, but also as permanent colour above.

The removal of single colours from the hair is similar to that of ordinary shampooing. However, special care should paid to removing colour around the hairline:

1. Sit the client at the basin and remove any caps, shoulder capes, etc.
2. Place a freshly laundered towel around the neck and across the shoulders.
3. Adjust the basin so that when the client's head is tilted back the position is comfortable with the minimum of towel supporting the neck.
4. Turn on the water and control the mixture of hot and cold. Test the temperature on the back of the hand to make sure it is neither too cold nor too hot. (Put on your gloves.)
5. Place one hand across the brow of the hairline, 'damming' the water from splashing forward onto the face. Start rinsing the hair from the forehead, down either side, cupping the ears and through to the lengths.
6. Check the flow of water pressure and temperature regularly throughout.
7. Colours will come off the hair easier if they are mulsified first. So, during the rinsing process and before any shampooing takes place, gently massage the scalp and hair so that the water mixes with the colour to form an emulsion. Rinse this away.
8. Apply a small amount of the correct shampoo to the palms of the hand, lightly rub together and then apply evenly to the client's hair.
9. With the fingers clawed, massage the scalp (using the appropriate massage technique); cover the whole scalp making sure that no areas are missed.
10. Rinse the hair thoroughly, checking water temperature and pressure.
11. If the stylist requires two washes, repeat steps 8–10.
12. Rinse all traces of shampoo lather away from the hair and lightly squeeze out the excess water.
13. Condition the hair in the usual way.

Rinsing the colour away

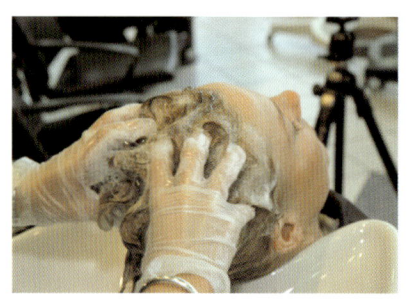

Apply shampoo and massage the scalp

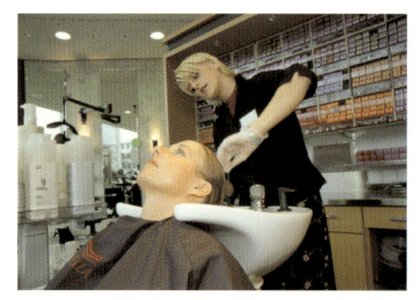

Rinse all traces of shampoo away and condition as usual

Removing (multiple) colours from hair

Removing multiple colours (e.g. high-lights) from the hair is a little more complex. Generally speaking, if two or more colours are introduced to the hair, they are packaged separately in some way and there are a number of reasons for this:

- Different colours need to be kept apart so that they don't merge together, forming an unwanted effect.
- Different colours often develop at different rates and therefore some might have been removed earlier than others.
- The colouring technique involves specific positioning or placement. This maximises colour impact by using the shape texture and style of the hair.
- Sometimes the client's hair colour needs correcting, perhaps because of a previous poor application or because it has discoloured.

You need to know how to recognise different colours within the hair and, when they are ready, be able to remove them carefully and safely.

Generally speaking, in high-lights where lighter and darker shades are involved it is easier to remove the darkest shade first, then the next darkest and so on. This is because there is more chance of darker colours running into lighter hair and ruining the effect. However, in certain cases, things are done the other way around.

Bleach is often used to lighten hair and, during high-lighting, certain areas can develop more readily than others; some sections will need to be removed earlier than others. The most important thing to remember is: if you don't know, ask. If the stylist tells you that colours need to be removed in specific order, there will be a reason.

Now try these out!

Activity

Example questions and model answers.

Q1 if you were neutralising a perm and during the rinsing stage a couple of curlers worked free. What do you do?

A1 I would inform the stylist immediately so that she could re-position them.

Q2 Why should you use latex gloves or barrier cream during neutralising?

A2 Because this operation involves chemicals that could affect the hands and even cause dermatitis

Q3 What should you do with used end papers, cotton wool and plastic caps?

A3 They should be disposed of immediately and not left around at the basins.

Q4 Why is the client's seating position so important during neutralising?

A4 It is particularly important the client is comfortable because neutralising takes a long time.

Activity

Perming and relaxing: a quiz to test your knowledge.

Q1 What does neutraliser do?
- ❏ It conditions the hair
- ❏ It fixes the curl in the hair
- ❏ It has no effect on the hair
- ❏ It breaks down the bonds in the hair

Q2 Why is timing so important during the application of neutraliser?
- ❏ It could overrun into lunch
- ❏ The lotion needs a minimum time to work
- ❏ It isn't, the lotion works immediately

Q3 Why is timing so important during the rinsing phase?
- ❏ Too much rinsing will reduce the perm result
- ❏ Too little rinsing will reduce the perm result
- ❏ The timing has no effect on the perm result

Q4 What is the minimum time for rinsing a perm on short, layered hair?
- ❏ 5 minutes
- ❏ 2 minutes
- ❏ 10 minutes
- ❏ 1 minute

Q5 What is the minimum time for rinsing a perm on longer, shoulder-length hair?
- ❏ 5 minutes
- ❏ 2 minutes
- ❏ 10 minutes
- ❏ 1 minute

Q6 In what form does the chemical Relaxer come in?
- ❏ Lotion
- ❏ Mousse
- ❏ Cream
- ❏ Gel

Q7 In what way does the Relaxer's neutraliser differ to perms?
- ❏ It doesn't differ – it's the same
- ❏ It does a different job
- ❏ It can be in a shampoo
- ❏ It can be in a conditioner

Activity

Colour and colour removal: a quiz to test your knowledge.

Q1 Why should you emulsify the colour before shampooing off? Because:
- ❏ It saves shampoo
- ❏ It saves conditioner
- ❏ It makes it easier to remove
- ❏ It make it stay on the hair better

Q2 When taking off high-lights, which colours are normally removed first?
- ❏ The mid-tone colour
- ❏ The darkest colour
- ❏ The lightest colour
- ❏ All at the same time

Q3 When taking off high-lights, which colours are normally removed last?
- ❏ The mid-tone colour
- ❏ The darkest colour
- ❏ The lightest colour
- ❏ All at the same time

Q4 What effect do you think bleach will have in a set of high-lights?
- ❏ It makes the hair lighter
- ❏ It makes the hair darker
- ❏ It makes the hair blue
- ❏ It makes the hair white

Q5 Which product is easier to rinse out of the hair?
- ❏ Semi-permanent colour
- ❏ Permanent colour
- ❏ Bleach
- ❏ High-lift tint

Q6 Who decides when a colour is ready for removal?
- ❏ You
- ❏ The stylist
- ❏ The manufacturer
- ❏ Te client

Activity

Now answer the following questions; ask your supervisor to check them.

Q1 Why are the manufacturer's instructions so important?
A1 ....

Q2 Why should you follow the stylist's instructions during neutralising or taking colours off?
A2 ....

Q3 During neutralising, what could happen if you used the wrong neutraliser?
A3 ....

Q4 What sort of problems do you think could happen during neutralising?
A4 ....

Q5 What sort of problems do you think could happen during colour removal?
A5 ....

Supervisor's signature: .... **Date:** ....

Activity

Now rate yourself on the checkerboard.

I know how to prepare clients correctly ☐	I know how to dispose of waste materials properly ☐	I know who and when to ask about chemical processes and procedures ☐	I know the salon's techniques for the chemical processes of neutralising and taking off colours ☐
I know how dermatitis can occur and how it is avoided ☐	I understand the implications of backwash product in relation to personal health and safety ☐	I always make sure clients are comfortable throughout the chemical processes ☐	I know how to communicate effectively with staff and customers ☐
I understand the implications of poor cleaning, tidiness and salon hygiene ☐	I understand the neutralising process and what could happen if I went wrong ☐	I always follow the stylist's instructions ☐	I understand the colour removing processes and what could happen if I went wrong ☐
I know why the wastage of salon resources should be minimised ☐	I know why timing is critical to the success of chemical processes ☐		**CHECKER BOARD ✓**

Appendix

General guidance on health and safety legislation applicable to hairdressing (Courtesy of HABIA)

Health and safety is the responsibility of everyone at work, although employers and supervisors in particular have a greater responsibility for health and safety than, say, the trainee stylist and/or stylist, but *all* have a responsibility to work in a healthy and safe manner.

Section 7 of the Health and Safety at Work Act of 1974 says:

> It shall be the duty of every employee while at work:
>
> **a** to take reasonable care for the health and safety of himself [sic] and of other persons who may be affected by his acts or omissions at work; and
>
> **b** as regard and duty or requirement imposed on the employer or under any of the relevant statutory provisions to co-operate with him so far as is necessary to enable that duty or requirement to be performed or complied with.

Many individual items of health and safety legislation apply to the working of a hairdressing salon. Some like 'The Management of Health & Safety at Work Regulations 1992' (which require management to carry out a risk assessment of the salon, to identify hazards and to improve working conditions and practices) obviously apply mainly to your employer. Other items of legislation apply to employers *and* all those working within the salon.

The following are the principal items of legislation that apply to general salon operations and, therefore, to employers *and* employees/trainees, etc., alike:

The Health and Safety at work etc. Act (1974): the great 'enabling' Act from which most of the subsequent legislation has sprung.

The Workplace (Health, Safety & Welfare) Regulations (1992): has taken the place of most of the Office, Shops and Railway Premises Act (1963), and require everyone at work to help maintain a safe and healthy working environment. They apply very much to the hairdressing salons.

Manual Handling Operations Regulations (1992): place upon everyone at work the duty to minimise the risks from lifting and handling objects.

The Provision and use of Work Equipment Regulations (1992): impose upon the employee the duty to select equipment for use at work that is properly constructed, suitable for the purpose and kept in good repair. Employers must also ensure that all who use the equipment have been adequately trained. The requirement for competence to use salon tools and equipment is embodied within the hairdressing standards.

The Personal Protective Equipment at Work Regulations (1992): confirm the requirement for employers to provide suitable and sufficient protective clothing/equipment, and for all employees to use it when required. The use of personal protective equipment (PPE) is a requirement of the hairdressing standards.

The Control of Substances Hazardous to Health Regulations (1992) (often referred to as COSHH) to include subsequent amendments: are particularly important as the storage, use and sale of a wide range of chemicals forms an important part of salon services, especially as such substances are applied on and sold to non-employees, i.e. clients.

The Electricity at Work Regulations (1989): under this law, your salon is required to maintain electrical equipment in a safe condition. It is your responsibility to report any faulty electrical equipment that you come across in your workplace.

Reporting of Injuries, Diseases and Dangerous Occurrences Regulations (1985) (often referred to as RIDDOR): under this regulation your salon is required to report injuries, disease and dangerous occurrences. It is your responsibility to report to the relevant person any injuries and dangerous occurrences that happen at work. Your salon might also require you to report any potentially infectious conditions of which you become aware.

Cosmetic Products (Safety) Regulations (1989): this law lays down rules for recommended volumes and strengths of different hydroxide-based products. The strength of a product will vary depending on whether it has been prepared for professional or non-professional general use. It is important that, when using these products, you check the strength against the manufacturer's guidance notes and check current legislation.

Copies of the regulations can be bought from her Majesty's Stationery Office (HMSO) bookshops. Guidance can also be obtained from individual manufacturers and the Hairdressing and Beauty Suppliers Association.

Glossary

access and egress	The ways of getting into and out of the building. *See* **evacuation procedures**.
appointment system	The fundamental system which organises the volume of work (client services or treatments) undertaken by a salon. This may be manual or computerised.
assessment	An evaluation or judgement of input, value and/or attainment.
assignment	A personal account or allocation of work, written, pictorial or practical based around clearly set objectives.
BD	Appointment abbreviation for Blow Dry
bleach	A hairdressing product that dissolves/removes natural colour pigments from hair.
body language	A non-verbal form of communication that infers the way a person is thinking or feeling.
case study	A study, examination or evaluation of specific event(s) either factual or hypothetical.
CBD	Appointment abbreviation for Cut & Blow Dry
client care	Providing service to salon customers in a way that promotes; good will, comfort, satisfaction and interest, which ultimately results in regular, client return visits.
client consultation	A service which is usually provided before the client has anything done to her hair. Consultation will find out what the client wants, identify any styling limitations, provide advise and maintenance information and formulate a plan of action.
Col (Rt or Fh)	Appointment abbreviation for Colouring (Root application or Full head)
Confidential information	May include personal aspects of conversations with clients or colleagues, contents of client records, client and staff personal details (e.g. address, telephone numbers, etc.) financial aspects of the business, hearsay/gossip.
Consumer and Retail Legislation	**The Consumer Protection Act (1987)** This Act follows European directives to protect the buyer from unsafe products. The Act is designed to help safeguard the consumer from products that do not reach reasonable levels of safety.

Consumer Protection (Distance Selling) Regulations 2000

These are derived from a European Directive and cover the supply of goods and/or services made between suppliers acting in a commercial capacity and consumers, i.e. an individual acting outside a trade business or profession. The regulations should be of concern to any individual purchasing goods or services by telephone, using the internet, digital television or mail order catalogues and conversely be of concern to any suppliers dealing with consumers through these media.

The Consumer Safety Act (1978)

There is a requirement to reduce the possible risk to consumers from any product that may be potentially dangerous.

The Prices Act (1974)

The price of products has to be displayed in order to prevent a false impression to the buyer.

The Trades Descriptions Act (1968 and 1972)

Products must not be falsely or misleadingly described in relation to its quality, fitness, price or purpose, by advertisements, orally, displays or descriptions. And since 1972 it is also a requirement to label a product clearly, so that the buyer can see where the product was made

The Resale Prices Act (1964 and 1976)

The manufacturers can supply a recommended price (MRRP), but the seller is not obliged to sell at the recommended price.

The Sale and Supply of Goods Act (1994)

The vendor must ensure that the goods they sell are of satisfactory quality, i.e. defined as the standard that would be regarded by a reasonable person of satisfactory having taken into account the description of the goods, the price and other relevant circumstances. Reasonably fit, i.e. ensuring that as a vendor that the goods can meet the purpose they are claimed to do.

cortex	The inner part of the hair where permanent colour is deposited and where perms make physical changes to the hair.
cross infection	The passing on of disease from one to another, either by contact or proximity, caused by poor hygiene and sanitation.
cuticle	The outer protective layers of the hair shaft.
database	An archive of information, usually held on computer, relating to business records, i.e. clients, staff, sales, products etc.
Data Protection Act	Under this act, you must not pass on any client or salon related information without the permission of the person involved. You have a duty of care to keep any such information safe and secure.
depth and tone	See **hair colour**.
dermis	The lower layers of newer skin below the outer epidermis.
dermatitis	A skin condition which results in a red, sore, hot and itchy rash,

Glossary

	usually between the fingers. This is sometimes caused by the contact of hairdressing chemicals and solutions.
double booking	An error in the appointment system where client's bookings overlap.
dry hair	A condition (usually the result of chemical treatments) in which the hair loses natural moisture levels, affecting the handling, maintenance and style durability.
epidermis	The older, upper, protective layers of skin at the surface.
evacuation procedures	The arrangements made by the salon i.e. exit route, assembly point, etc., for emergency purposes.
follicle	A 'tube'-like indentation within the skin, from which the hair grows.
greasy hair	A condition caused by the over production of natural oils, i.e. sebum, which exudes from glands within the scalp on to the surface and eventually the hair. Thus affecting the handling, maintenance and style durability
hair colour	The resultant effect from two colour aspects 1) **depth** – the lightness or darkness of a colour and 2) **tone** – the degree of red, gold, ash, etc., within the hair.
hair texture	Texture refers to the 'thickness or thinness' of individual hairs i.e. course, medium, fine etc.
hair tendency	Tendency refers to straightness, wave, body, curl or frizzyness.
HL	Appointment abbreviation for High-lighting.
HL T sect	Appointment abbreviation for High-light top and sides only.
layering (layered cut)	A cutting technique carried out on either short or long hair to produce a multi-length effect.
legal requirements	This refers to laws affecting the way businesses are operated, how the salon or workplace is set up and maintained, people in employment and the systems of working which must be maintained.
manufacturer instructions	Explicit guidance issued by manufacturers or suppliers of products or equipment, concerning their safe and efficient use.
massage techniques	*effleurage* — a gentle stroking movement *petrissage* — slow, firm kneading movement *friction* — a stimulating, vigorous rubbing movement using the finger pads.
neutraliser	The second chemical (re-bonding) phase for perming or relaxing hair. *See* **permanent wave – relaxing**.
NVQs	National Vocational Qualification.
one length cut	A cutting technique where the hair is cut with the natural hair fall to produce a one-length effect.
overbooking	*See* **double booking**.

permanent tint (permanent colour)	A penetrating colour product that adds synthetic pigments to natural hair until it grows out.
perm solution	The first part of a permanent wave system which chemically modifies the hair's inner structure.
permanent wave (perm)	A two-part system for adding movement to hair by chemical means.
personal presentation	This includes; personal hygiene, use of personal protective equipment, clothing and accessories suitable to the particular workplace.
personal protective equipment (PPE)	You are required to use and wear the appropriate protective equipment during perming, colouring and relaxing services or in any situation where personal harm may be encountered.
potentially infectious condition	A medical condition or state of health which may be transmitted to others. *See* **cross infection**.
porous hair	Hair that has lost surface protection, therefore having a greater absorption and less resistance to chemicals and products. This affects the hair's manageability, handling, and ability to hold in a style. *See* **dry hair**.
portfolio	A system for recording experiences, case studies, personal accounts, results from tests/assessments and the findings from projects and assignments.
project	Similar to an assignment.
PU	Appointment abbreviation for 'Put up', i.e. longer hair dressed up for party, ball or bridal occasions.
PW	Appointment abbreviation for Permanent wave (Perm).
quasi permanent colours	Colour products which should be treated as permanent colours in terms of application, testing and future services.
relaxing	A chemical process (usually in two parts) which removes natural movement/curl from hair.
reshape (reshaping)	Cutting hair back into style. (A six-weekly reshape cut will maintain a hairstyle.)
restyle	Cutting hair into a new hairstyle.
resources	Anything used to enable the delivery and completion of service to the client (e.g. people, equipment stock)
responsible persons	A term used, particularly in Health and Safety to mean the person(s) at work, whom you should report any issues, problems or hazards. This could be a supervisor, line manager or your employer.
role plays	A simulation of events to evaluate communication between people.
salon requirements	Any hairdressing procedures or work rules issued by the salon management.

scalp	The skin covering the top of the head.
stock check (stock taking)	An accounting process for monitoring and controlling the movements and usage of stock.
temporary colour	Colour added to hair, that lasts until the next wash.
tint and tinting	The professional term for colour and colouring. *See* **hair colour**.
trimming hair	*See* **reshape, reshaping**.
verify (verifier)	A person responsible for quality assurance within a training scheme, who makes sure that candidates and staff are working to the correct standards.
workplace policies	This covers the documentation prepared by your employer on the procedures to be followed in your workplace.
WC	Appointment abbreviation for Wet cutting.

Index

accidents 29
African-Caribbean hair 104–106, 114, 116–117
ammonium thioglycolate 110
antiperspirants 25
antiseptics 78
appearance (personal) 24–25
appointments 37–38, 49–53, 60
    booking error 51
    diary 40
    system 34, 49
appraisals 66–69
assessment 5–6
    risk 13, 78
autoclaves 77

bacteria 76
Barbicide® 77
barrier cream 21
body
    language 49
    odour (BO) 24

clothes 24
colour
    processes 103–108, 110–111
    correction 119
    removal 117–119
    retouch 107
communication (client) 43–47, 55, 58–59
    non-verbal 45–46
computer records 87
conditioner 95–96
    application technique 99–100
    surface 99
confidentiality 34, 47

COSHH regulations 9, 13, 19, 126
Cosmetic Products Regulations (1989) 126
cross-infection 74
curlers 109, 114
customer care 34, 36, 58–59
cuticle (hair) 94

dandruff 96
Data Protection Act 60, 87
deodorants 25
dermatitis 22, 93
discoloration 119
disentangling hair 100
disinfection 78
disulphide bonds 110, 113

effective communication 34
efficiency and effectiveness 39
effleurage (hair massage) 90, 99
Electricity at Work Regulations (1989) 126
element (NVQ) 4
emergencies 28
equipment
    hand-held 84

fire 28
first aid 29
first impressions 39
floors (cleaning) 80
follicle (hair) 94
friction hair massage 90, 99
fungi 76

good impression 58
goodwill 57

Index

hair
    course 95
    disentangling 100
    disulphide bonds 110
    dry/porous 95
    fine 95
    greasy 95
    manageability 90
    massage 99
    structure 94
    type/texture 95
halitosis 24
hands 21–22
hazards 8, 12–15
head lice 20
Health and Safety 7–32, 125–126
    at Work Act (1974) 8–9, 125
    law 19, 125–126
high-lights 107, 119
hood dryers and colour accelerators, 83
hydrogen peroxide 110
hygiene
    personal 21–24
    salon 79

infection 19–20
    prevention 76
injuries (reporting regulations) 126

jewellery 25

knowledge and understanding (NVQ) 4

lice (head) 20
lighteners 117
low-lights 107

mandatory units (NVQ) 2–3
Manual Handling Operations Regulations (1992) 126
mirrors (cleaning) 83
mouth 24

nails 21
National Vocational Qualification (NVQ) 4
neutraliser 107, 109–110
nits 20

obstructions (working environment) 17
optional units (NVQ) 2–3

pathogens 76
performance criteria (NVQ) 4
permanent tint 107, 117
perms 103–115
personal
    action (training) plans 69
    appearance 24–25
    hygiene 21–24
    protective equipment (PPE) 15, 22, 126
    reviews 68
petrissage (hair massage) 90, 99
pityriasis simplex (dry dandruff) 96
posture 25–26
powder bleach 107
products (salon) 39–41, 114
    information 41
professional communication 39, 49

range (NVQ) 4
reception duties 33–39
records (client) 59, 87
relaxing processes 103–108, 110, 116
retail areas 36–43
risks 8, 15
    assessment 13
rods 109
role play 39
root (hair) 94
rotary hair massage 90, 99

salon duties and routines 73–88
self
    appraisal 68
    development 69
    directed learning 5
semi-permanent colour 107, 117
shampooing and conditioning 89–102
    preparations 92–94
    technique 96–99
shoes 25
solutions
    acidic 114
    alkaline 114
spillages 17, 80
steatoid pityriasis (greasy dandruff) 96
sterilisation 74, 76–78
strengths and weaknesses 67

styling
    mirrors 83
    tools 83
surface tension 92
SWOT analysis 68

taking messages 47
teamwork 63
telephone answering 45, 47–48
temporary colour 120
test curl 109
time management 63
towels and gowns 83
trolleys/trays (preparation) 79

ultraviolet (UV) radiation 77

viruses 76
visual impressions 45

waste
    disposal 85
    'sharp' 85
work surfaces 81
working relationships 55–58, 63–65
Workplace Regulations (1992) 126

yeast (in dandruff) 96